The Naked Teacher

How to Survive Your First Five Years in Teaching

The Naked Teacher

How to Survive Your First Five Years in Teaching

Louisa Leaman

continuum
LONDON • NEW YORK

Continuum International Publishing Group

The Tower Building   80 Maiden Lane
11 York Road   Suite 704
London   New York
SE1 7NX   NY 10038

www.continuumbooks.com

British Library Cataloguing-in-Publication data
A catalogue record for this book is available from the British Library.

ISBN: 0-8264-8540-5 (paperback)

Library of Congress Cataloging-in-Publication Data
A catalog record for this book is available from the Library of Congress.

Typeset by Servis Filmsetting Ltd, Manchester
Printed and bound in Great Britain by
Antony Rowe Ltd, Chippenham, Wiltshire

Contents

Part Two: What does Training Involve?

Part Three: Coping with Your First Job

Survival

Part Four: Valuable Personality Traits

Introduction

So you have decided teaching is the career for you. Welcome to the exciting world of education – no really, it *is* exciting. It's not just about marking and coffee mugs, you know. Well, maybe the caffeine fix *is* quite important – but as you will quickly discover there is much more to it. Fight scenes that would rival your average action movie, romantic tensions across crowded rooms, language you never knew existed, laughter, tears, tyranny . . . and that's just the staffroom. If you ever dare to venture out of it you will realize there is a world of excitement waiting to be discovered – corridors that no one told you about (cover duty will lead you to some remote classroom in a department you never heard of), challenges for you to confront heroically (GCSE moderation? For the entire year group? In two hours? Fetch me my red pen!) and, of course, there is always something exciting going on at lunchtime (table tennis tournaments, mass 'bundles', French club). Oh, and there are children. Everywhere. Lots of them.

Is it any wonder teachers rarely complain of boredom? They may complain about many things, but feeling under-stretched is not one of them. So with all the adventure and activity that takes place within the confines of a school, how does the earnest, humble teacher manage to stay on top of the game? *The Naked Teacher* will, I hope, help to answer that question, and strip away the layers of doubt and confusion. It is designed to provide down-to-earth guidance through the maze of responsibilities, challenges and expectations that under-pin a successful first five years in the profession. Whether you are a curious outsider contemplating a career change, a newly qualified teacher (NQT) just 'starting out', or a more experienced practitioner looking to make the most of your developing skills – this book is for you. It outlines what you have to do, explains why you have to do it, and gives practical advice on how to do it well.

The book is divided into three sections. The first, Getting Started, establishes an overview of the job requirements and training process. The second section, Survival, explores what it takes to cope with the first few years of teaching: how to get to grips with the basics, minimize the problems, overcome challenges and succeed in managing that highly important education commodity: other people. The third section, Beyond Survival, is (as the title suggests) intended to shine a guiding light for those who feel they have conquered the battle for survival and now want to thrive: information and advice on how to improve classroom practice, avoid stagnation and climb the ranks of professional hierarchy.

The information is based on what I wish I had known as I made those first tenuous steps towards my own classroom door. My career started like many others – a post-university panic response to the question 'What do I do now?' I had some naive ideas that teaching might be 'fun', and 'interesting', and low on time consumption (short working days, endless weeks of holiday). Ho-hum. Needless to say it has asked more from me than I ever expected.

What it *has* been is a fast-paced, satisfying and mentally stimulating whirlwind of experiences. There have been highs and lows, twists and turns, moments of clarity, and many more of frustration. But as I reflect on my career to date – which has taken me from large comprehensive secondaries to tiny independent special schools, from gifted and talented A level candidates to enraged 6-year-olds with ADHD (attention deficit and hyperactivity disorder), from charming deputy heads to sociopathic curriculum coordinators – I realize how much I have learned about my job, and myself. It is great to have the opportunity to share this insight, and to help others get the most from this potentially rewarding profession.

Getting started

Part One

What do Teachers do?

Teach, surely? Well, yes, they do teach, but this is actually a euphemism for a million and one different tasks and responsibilities. The information in this part of the book is concerned with shedding light on some of these tasks and responsibilities. It is not an exhaustive list, but outlines the key activities that a classroom teacher is involved with: the basic things you should expect to be doing in order to fulfil your role – but as those who have been in teaching for some time might agree, there is always more to do if you are keen!

If you have already had some experience in the classroom, the job description will be familiar to you. If you are new or contemplating joining the profession, the following information may seem quite daunting. I cannot lie – there is a lot of responsibility to get to grips with. But I can assure you that if you are patient with yourself and your experiences it will eventually fall into place.

Perhaps the most important areas of responsibility you will have can be regarded as the management of learning, of behaviour and of the classroom itself. None of these things stand alone: successful learning absorbs student attention, therefore reducing problematic behaviour; effective behaviour management stabilizes the atmosphere, enabling the students – and you – to focus on learning; and if all of this is done in a classroom that is well ordered and pleasant everything becomes easier.

In addition to your role within the classroom you will find you have a number of significant tasks within the wider realm of the school – many of which are vital to its effectiveness. It is common practice for teachers to complain endlessly about breaktime duty, and to bemoan anything that involves staying late, such as meetings or parents' evenings – but these are all cogs in the school's busy clockworks. If done effectively, they give rise to a smooth, efficient working environment. Recognizing your role within the whole school can also be quite refreshing. A teacher's life is fairly isolated – alone for hours among a sea of other people's children – but the rest of the adult population is just on the other side of your classroom door. Make the most of opportunities to interact, to collaborate and to remind yourself that you have comrades.

1 Managing learning

Subject knowledge

Inspiration to teach stems from the desire to share knowledge – it stands to reason that a teacher needs to possess knowledge before they are able to share it. The chances are you have chosen to teach a subject that you have studied substantially, and are wildly enthusiastic about – therefore you are already on the right track. However, it is not simply a matter of having the knowledge, but of knowing what to do with it. Here are some hints on how to share your subject knowledge effectively:

- Unleash your own enthusiasm and sell your subject. If you talk up a topic and express how it interests you, your students will be swept along with you.
- Capture their imagination. Pick up on the obscure, quirky or gory aspects of your subject matter, and use these to surprise or shock.
- Put facts into human context. Promote a piece of information by making it seem relevant to the lives of your students – sometimes mundane details are the things that intrigue us the most.
- Invite students to challenge your opinion, or that of the textbook.
- Ask 'open' questions (ones without yes/no responses), to encourage broader exploration of a topic or issue.
- Share anecdotes and tales of your own studies; for example your chance encounter with a famous professor, your exciting field trip to the Amazon, or your journey back in time to Renaissance Italy.

Knowing how to use your knowledge can make for inspiring teaching, but what if you do not feel you have quite the necessary knowledge in mind? After all, this is the real world: not all teachers get to teach subjects they like all of the time, particularly those of a primary persuasion. I battled with year 6 numeracy for long enough to know how *that* feels. Within a particular subject, the curriculum may require you to teach an area you are unfamiliar with. And for those joining the profession after years in the workforce, opening up a textbook may feel somewhat alien – ten years of corporate fundraising has little to do with the breeding cycle of frogs. Here are some tips if you have to teach something you are not too sure about, or feel that your brainpower is a little rusty:

- Do your homework. Read up and around the subject as much as you can – with the advent of the Internet there is little excuse not to find information and renew your confidence.
- Look through textbooks and attempt to answer relevant questions/complete tasks yourself – this will give you a good rehearsal, and help you to understand the processes your students will need to go through in order to do the work.
- Acquaint yourself with the curriculum, which will allow you to grasp a basic insight into what needs to be covered.
- Make sure you know the course/exam syllabus – this will help you to focus your teaching and provide the essentials.
- Put in a request for helpful training opportunities or courses.
- Ask for support. Maybe another member of your department can give you a few pointers, or share their planning with you.

Planning and preparation

For the student teacher, a thorough planning sheet can feel like a security blanket. My own experience of teacher training led me to believe that they were the most important documents in the world. Writing them, however, always seemed to take up inordinate amounts of time, and considering I barely managed to glance at one during those frenetic early lessons, it all seemed rather unbalanced. By the end of my first year as a fully qualified teacher I rebelled against the planning process and abandoned it altogether – and that is when I learned the true value of planning! Without it, my lessons

seemed to sag and go nowhere. My students lost direction, started
to act up, and I quickly lost my footing.

Effective planning is the key to a tightly run classroom. It under-
pins a lesson with structure and focus, and helps both you and your
students to reach the intended goal. Obviously there are certain
hoops to be jumped through during times of training and Ofsted
but, beyond this, good planning is an individual process. Make it
work for you:

- Use a planning format, making it quicker to write and easier
  to interpret. If this can be available on a computer you will
  save even more time (and storage).
- Treat it as a working document. Make sure it is easily accessible, and use it in the classroom. Note changes, successes and
  difficulties – helping you to keep track of student progress.
- Avoid too much detail or superfluous information – you will
  only be wasting your time. Planning should inform and direct
  what happens in the classroom, not prescribe it.
- If in doubt, trust that in time you will find your own planning rhythm. As your classroom confidence increases your
  planning, and the time it takes, will refine.
- Plan in context. If you follow the guidelines for long-,
  medium- and short-term planning (see below) you will always
  know where you are heading.
- Start with aims. Decide what you want your students to
  achieve by the end of the lesson, and select activities and tasks
  that will lead them there.
- Keep your aims in mind when delivering the lesson. This will
  help you to monitor and assess student progress, and recognize whether the lesson is working or not.
- Remain flexible. There will be times when best-laid plans are
  disrupted. If a fire alarm wipes out half of your lesson time
  you may need to rethink last minute.
- Keep everything. Especially medium/long-term planning
  that can be reused.
- Streamline. If you teach several classes in the same year group,
  teach them the same scheme of work. Adjust your short-term
  planning per class, in order to make it interesting for you and
  to take account of different student needs.

There are three different levels of planning that can enable you to organize your lessons throughout the year. You may be able to coordinate the cycle of topics with the rest of your department or year group, and perhaps even spread the workload between you.

- *Long-term planning*: This is your annual cycle of topics. In consultation with National Curriculum documentation, decide what topics and themes need to be covered for each term, taking into account exam preparation and coursework requirements, and block them into termly/half-termly slots. This will enable you to establish a clear cycle of progression, and to prepare ahead of yourself.
- *Medium-term planning*: This can be done at the start of every half-term/term, and is a more in-depth account of the topics outlined in the long-term plan. Medium-term planning can be the outline of a 'scheme of work', providing brief week-by-week indications of the key aims that need to be addressed. Again, this can be done with your department and allows you to prepare in advance for the term ahead of you, and to structure the pace and content of a project to ensure that everything necessary is included.
- *Short-term planning*: This is a more detailed breakdown of individual lessons, and can be done on a weekly, or even daily, basis. It could include the lesson objectives, key vocabulary, tasks to be undertaken (including details of textbooks, page references, discussion topics, types of activity, differentiated tasks), assessment criteria and homework. In other words it should contain enough information to enable another teacher to pick it up and understand what is going on.

Differentiation

A key part of managing the learning process is making the learning objectives accessible to all. By this I mean presenting information in ways that can be understood by students of varying abilities, and providing tasks that are appropriate to the needs of the most and least capable. This is differentiation. It is a tough challenge. The prospect of planning a fabulous scheme of work, then adjusting your planning several times over in order to cater for five different learning styles, four gifted and talented, three English as an Additional Language (EAL), two specific learning disorders and one autistic student is hard. But before you hang up your mortarboard with resigned weariness remind yourself that the benefits of effective differentiation *are* significant, and will undoubtedly outweigh the effort required. If work is pitched at the right level and provides a suitable amount of challenge students will:

- remain on task for longer periods
- be less reliant on teacher intervention and support
- be less likely to get drawn into inappropriate behaviour
- develop self-esteem and confidence as learners
- have increased motivation
- make faster progress.

Of course, in the average classroom it is not feasible to set individual work for every student, but it may be helpful to establish different groupings of ability such as low, middle and high. These groupings could be 'virtual' (students are spread out throughout the class) or literal (students of similar ability are seated together). In most classrooms the largest group is likely to be that of middle ability students – pitch the overall lesson at this level, and then provide simplified/extended versions of tasks for the other groups. You may be responsible for students with significant learning difficulties, with abilities that fall outside of your general groupings. Their work will need to be differentiated further. If you are unsure, seek advice from your special educational needs coordinator.

Differentiation requires good organizational skills. If this is your forte you may thrive on developing a buzzing classroom where several different activities are going on at once. This will certainly be made easier if you have additional adult support in your room. Here are a few extra tips:

- Look out for low literacy skills as this may mean students are unable to cope with large amounts of independent writing, and will struggle to read or follow instructions.
- Understand that some students will work at a slower rate, not because they are lazy but because it takes them more time to absorb and process information.

- Differentiation is not just about adjusting tasks; it is also about adjusting expectations. You will know what you want the majority of your students to achieve by the end of a lesson or project; think too about what you want the less able individuals to achieve and set goals that are appropriate for them.

- Decide what you want the learning outcomes to be and adjust tasks to fit these. If you are looking for a demonstration of knowledge and understanding, is it necessary for unconfident writers to produce pages of writing, when the task of writing itself may prove too much?

- Provide key vocabulary lists (either on the board or as a separate handout), word banks/dictionaries, wide-ruled lined paper for those who have difficulties with handwriting, and writing frameworks (guidelines for planning, structuring and organizing written work).

- Be specific about the minimum amount of work you expect your students to complete and in what amount of time, and remember to adjust your expectations accordingly – one child's two sentences is another child's three pages!

- Give clear instructions. Ask students to repeat them back to you, in order to check their understanding, or write them on the board as a visual reminder.

- Adapt worksheets. If they are computerized this should not be a major headache. Keep a copy of whatever you produce and it can then be reused, saving time in the future.

- Use colour-coded bookmarks to keep track of useful textbook material: for example, green for easy tasks, orange for medium and red for difficult. This idea could be extended to the colour of paper your worksheets are copied on – making it easier to recognize what is what.

- Have a back-up supply of extension tasks to challenge the minds of the brighter students, should they finish their work ahead of time. These could include independent research activities or more complicated versions of the work they have just completed.

- If suitable, allow students access to computer technology. Computers are an effective means of removing barriers to learning, and can often motivate the more reluctant individuals.

Progression

Classroom satisfaction does not come just from giving out knowledge and information, but in seeing students take that knowledge and information and make sense of it. Helping a young person's mind to develop is not just a romantic classroom ideal. It is something that can be structured into your teaching in a very real and practical way: plan for progression. Of course, getting students to make the journey from A to B can be a daunting prospect for both you and them, but if you can provide milestones along the way the journey will be easier.

Know where your students are at, and where you want to get them to. Establish the steps they need to go through in order to get there, and then use this to inform your planning and lesson content. The 'steps' are the basis of what and how your students learn. Take, for example, the task of writing an essay: what would you need to know about in order to do it successfully?

1. Techniques for gathering and preparing ideas – brainstorming, making notes, spider diagrams and other planning aids, researching relevant information.
2. Forming an argument – establishing key points, finding comparisons, looking at different viewpoints, selecting examples and supporting evidence.
3. Organizing the information – writing in paragraphs, structuring main points, using introductions and conclusions, addressing the title and answering the question.
4. Writing style – formal writing conventions, consistency and clarity, using quotations and evidence, making it interesting, accurate grammar and spelling, exploring vocabulary.

If you are able to address each of these aspects adequately your chances of producing a successful piece of work are increased. If you are unaware, or struggle with any of them, the end result will be affected. Having an awareness of the different components of successful writing enables you to recognize what you are expected to achieve, and allows you to comprehend it in smaller sections, rather than one large and overwhelming task.

Apply this principle to your teaching: if your students develop a step-by-step understanding of information and activities, in which they are able to get to grips with small, manageable chunks of knowledge before putting them all together, they will have a greater chance of succeeding. Here are some suggestions for incorporating progression into your planning:

- *Begin with aims*: Decide what you want your students to achieve by the end of the term/scheme of work/week/lesson, and then plan steps towards that goal.
- *Use scaffolding*: Ensure that students have a sound understanding of the basic principles of what they are doing, and then build upon this. Start with a small idea and then expand it. This is the principle that guides progression through the National Curriculum, but it can also be used effectively in individual lessons.
- *Model what you want your students to do*: Step-by-step, whole-class, teacher-led demonstrations are an effective way of making knowledge explicit and clarifying what needs to be done. If students have already been led through an example they will have a greater chance of getting it right when they come to do it independently.
- *Revisit old ground*: Some students will have difficulty developing new skills or absorbing information in one take. Make regular opportunities to revisit knowledge, in order to reinforce the message. Keep it interesting by using different approaches and formats, for example a quick-fire round of oral questions, asking students to brainstorm everything they remember about a subject, using kinaesthetic strategies or studying visual material.
- *Set targets*: Setting targets for the whole class or for individuals can help you and your students to focus on progress. Keep them simple, achievable and time measured, for example: 'By the end of the week, we will be able to . . . remember our 6× table/label the parts of a cell/talk about the plot of *Romeo and Juliet*.'
- *Communicate your intentions*: Talk clearly to students about what you expect them to achieve, giving regular reminders and encouragement. Make the aims of each lesson explicit by writing them on the board or even asking students to copy them into their books. This will minimize ambiguity and

confusion, while encouraging students to focus their attention at the start of a lesson.

Assessment

Progression and assessment are closely linked. Without effective assessment of student need and ability it is difficult to establish appropriate expectations for progression. Find out where your students are starting from, and keep track of their development. Assessment has become de rigueur for teachers of all subjects and age groups. But it need not be overly onerous, and it can have a significant impact on your grasp of your students, helping you to make classwork accessible and meaningful for them, as well as identifying any gaps in their knowledge. It is also rewarding to discover hard evidence that your students have actually learned something!

Accurate assessment is not something that new teachers are automatically accustomed to. It can take time to develop an understanding of the curriculum and the nature of learning, before being able to dissect and evaluate it. Seek guidance from your colleagues/mentors, and try not to worry – you are probably spending enough time assessing your own performance, let alone anyone else's! In the meantime, here are some useful ideas:

- *Know your criteria*: Keep in mind the aims and objectives of your lesson plans – these will help to define what you are looking for. If you incorporate National Curriculum guidelines into your lesson aims then your assessment will fall in line.
- *Find short cuts to recording information*: Using codes or symbols can be a time-saving way of keeping track of progress. At the end of each lesson or project (depending on what is manageable), fill in a simple grid square for each student: a complete triangle means the student has fully understood the objective, two sides of a triangle means some understanding of the objectives, one side means little understanding, a circle means absent.
- *Marking class/homework*: Feeding back to your students is an essential part of the teaching process:
  - Suitable comments can be more purposeful than grades.
  - Highlight what should be improved or changed, but make sure the positives are emphasized.

- If you make value judgements ensure that they are specific, so that the student knows what they being praised or criticized for. Smiley face stickers may be motivating, but do not provide the explicit advice that can help children improve.
- Provide a target for the next piece of work.
- Develop a marking code for signalling spelling and grammatical mistakes.
- On occasion, ask students to mark their own/each other's work. This may help them to examine their own strengths and weaknesses.
- Provide oral feedback for a change.
- Make a note of common errors and misunderstandings, and go over these during the next lesson.
- Keep a record of tasks and their outcomes, including National Curriculum level indicators (once you are familiar with these).

- *Informal assessment methods*: You can make general observations regarding the progress of your students in several ways:
  - asking questions at the end of the lesson
  - a show of hands from students who think they understand
  - asking students to restate something in their own words
  - discussing work on a one-to-one basis
  - the general response of students to a task or project.
- *Formal assessment methods*: Structuring regular formal assessments into your planning can help you to stay on top of the assessment process. This can be done in conjunction with the rest of your department/year group, in order to establish consistency:
  - written tests
  - oral tests
  - timed essays
  - practical activities
  - presentations
- *Draw comparisons*: When trying to evaluate the work of a class or year group, the easiest way to start is by placing the best and worst at opposite ends of a table, and then ranking the rest in between (this can also be helpful when marking homework). It is also important to understand progress in the context of

individual achievement – you may wish to compare a student's recent work with their previous efforts.

- *Make use of the information*: Keep efficient records of your assessments, and you will find they serve a purpose in a number of ways. They can be whipped out at parents' evenings, marathon report writing sessions, and SEN (special educational needs) review meetings. Plus, the DfES seems to have a liking for them.

2 Managing behaviour

In the classroom

Bad behaviour? We can talk about it, argue about it and theorize about it until our tongues fall out, but surely the best thing is to *do* something about it? Dealing with difficult behaviour is a major concern for many teachers, and an issue that courts much political, public and media attention. Conversations with those curious about joining the profession suggest many people are put off by the fear of rowdy, uncontrollable students. But problems with behaviour vary from school to school, and are dependent on a number of factors. It is not as straightforward as 'large, inner city comprehensive in deprived area = violence and chaos' versus 'small, independent school with selective intake = model children'. I have had experience in a variety of different types of school, and have come to realize that the real key to maintaining good discipline is the attitude and approach of the staff, regardless of student intake and geographical location. So what is it that makes for effective teacher attitude and approach?

- A positive view of *all* students and their potential for appropriate behaviour.
- A calm, assertive manner when dealing with difficulties.
- Clear expectations/boundaries that are consistently and rigorously reinforced.
- A disciplinary approach that is firm but fair.
- A genuine desire for change and improvement.

Classrooms that are governed by strong behaviour management have a stable, positive atmosphere: one that can be maintained or quickly reasserted if difficulties do arise. It can, however, take time and concentrated effort to establish this status quo – if you work in a tough school, be prepared to repeat yourself constantly, grind your teeth with frustration, and forsake a third of your energy. Your students may indulge in repeated attempts to 'test' your mettle, but if you continue to plough they *will* get the message. Of course, this process will have to be revisited each time you encounter a new class, but eventually your reputation will leak out: someone knows someone's brother who was taught by you last year, and apparently you are 'well safe'!

I believe behaviour management has three significant levels of practice: preventive, reactive and follow-up. If you invest in the preventive level (methods intended to minimize the likelihood of problems arising or going too far) you will reduce the overall occurrence of difficult behaviour. If an incident does occur, there is a range of reactive strategies that can be used to address the situation, and then follow-up measures to ensure that everyone moves on.

Preventive:

- *Know your students*: Familiarize yourself with information about those with SEN (individual education plans (IEPs), statements, reports, comments from parents, SENCO and support staff), and seek advice from other teachers about the strategies they have found successful with the student(s) in question.
- *Take time to observe*: It sometimes pays to step back on occasion and watch the dynamics of the classroom. In doing this you can learn a lot about how your students interact with one another and what makes them tick.
- *Identify possible triggers*: Through observation you may discover that certain situations are a cause of difficult behaviour for some individuals, for example certain students sitting together, dislike of a task or particular comments made by you or another child. Recognizing these triggers will help you to avoid or prepare for their impact.
- *Anticipate the next move*: Vigilance is vital in the successful classroom. It will not take long to get to know the ways and habits of most of your students – many of them will be keen to show you! Keep a subtle eye on the mood of the class or particular individuals, and remain one step ahead of them.

- *Intervene early*: Small issues can quickly escalate into big ones when they are allowed to evolve. If you smell a rat, catch it straight away! If you are vigilant (as above) you will know what is happening in your room, and be able to step in when necessary so as to nip a potential problem in the bud.
- *Create a positive, welcoming atmosphere*: If your students feel valued and respected they are more likely to enjoy being in your classroom, even if they are not wild about your subject. If they enjoy being in your classroom they are less likely to want to spoil that experience.
- *Set clear boundaries*: Know what you are expecting from your students and then clearly communicate your expectations to them. If boundaries are explicit and regularly reinforced students will know where they stand.
- *Speak assertively*: Get into the habit of phrasing your classroom/behaviour management instructions as commands, rather than questions. 'I *want* you to . . .' or 'You *need* to . . .' is more emphatic than 'Can you please try to . . .?' Be polite, but be direct: make it clear that you are in command.
- *Acknowledge and reward good behaviour*: When your students get it right, ensure they know about it. Give regular praise (but not over-praise) and use a reward system (points/merits/stickers/star charts/etc.) that allows recognition of individual effort and achievement.

Reactive:

- *Verbal warnings*: Use a calm, clear and firm voice, with direct instructions about what the student is doing wrong, what they should be doing, and what will happen if they continue (the consequence of their actions). Two warnings will suffice – the biggest mistake teachers make is giving too many warnings without enacting the consequence.
- *Language of choice*: Experience has taught me that students are much more likely to cooperate if they feel they still have some control over the situation. Use phrases such as: 'You need to . . . or you will have to . . .' or 'If you . . . then you can . . .' Explain to the student that they have a choice, and that the

choice they make will lead to either a positive or negative consequence for them.

- *Allow for 'take-up' time*: If you give a student an instruction/ warning, give them a reasonable amount of time to carry out your request before you get on their case again. I often see problems evolving from teachers being too hasty and impatient in terms of their expectations (giving an instruction, then shouting at the student immediately after), which is perceived by the student as unfair.
- *Be repetitive*: When issuing a boundary warning or giving a student a choice, stick with it. They may not instantly co-operate, but do not be tempted to jump to another line of 'telling off': this may signal to them that you will not see things through. Stick with your expectations, repeat and reassert them. (Refusal to co-operate can then be dealt with as a separate issue.)
- *Time-out*: Offering students time-out (time and space to calm down, think about a problem, and reflect) can be an effective way of curbing difficult outbursts, and encouraging students to get control of their anger and aggression. It can also remove the oxygen of attention, which for many children is a trigger to escalating behavioural problems. Time-out should last no more than five minutes, in a quiet space away from the rest of the class. Though generally used for primary-aged students, I have administered it for teenagers with great success.
- *Consequences*: Focus on consequences to actions rather than punishment. They should be appropriate to the crime, consistently applied and followed up by whoever sets them. They could include detention, referral to a senior teacher, making apologies, completing a relevant activity (e.g. litter picking, helping another teacher or student, attending a homework club), a phone call home, a comment in the student's planner/diary, loss of privileges or going 'on report'.
- *Remove the problem*: A quick way to tackle a difficulty is to find the cause and remove it. This could be an item that students are squabbling over (look after it until the end of the lesson), or a student who is winding up others (send them on a time-out or to another area of the classroom).

- *Keep it simple.* If you have the support of colleagues when dealing with an incident, make sure only one of you does the talking. Too many voices can confuse the issue, or make the student feel as though they are being caged in. It is usually more helpful to have other people 'available' than to have them fully involved.

Follow-up:

- *Apologies*: Encouraging students to say sorry for difficult behaviour is an important part of the responsibility-taking process. Of course, this only means something if the apology is sincere. Do not accept apologies from students who are not able to explain what they are sorry for, look you in the eye, or keep a straight, solemn face – but be aware that some students may need time to calm down before they are able to face this task. I often use the phrase: 'When you are ready to apologize properly, I'm ready to listen.' As they tend to want attention and acceptance, they pull themselves together.
- *Praise improvements*: If, after receiving a warning or using time-out, a student successfully reforms their behaviour, express your appreciation. Discreetly tell them you are pleased they have chosen to do the 'right thing' – make them feel good about being good.
- *Seeing through consequences*: If you set a consequence you will need to ensure that the student faces up to it. If students believe you are true to your word they will be wary of misbehaving. If they think you are one for empty threats they will take advantage. Make sure your consequences are reasonable for both the student, and you, to achieve. Do you really want to enforce whole-class detention every day for a month?
- *A fresh start*: If an individual has done their best to destroy your carefully planned lesson it can be hard to let go of resentment. However, if you cannot move on, the student will not be able to move on either. I always remind students that once apologies have been made and consequences have been addressed the problem is finished with. I tell them that they now have the opportunity to show me how helpful and cooperative they

can be, and that I am looking forward to some positive lessons with them. This acceptance has had considerable results – with some extremely disaffected young people.

- *Reflective*: No matter what stage you are at in your teaching career there is always room to learn. Much can be gained from looking back over an incident and reflecting on how your interventions affected the outcome. What did and did not help? What was hard? What was easy? How did the student react? How did you react?
- *Seek further intervention*: If problematic behaviour has been of a serious nature, or is an ongoing problem despite your efforts, it will be necessary to take it further. Speak to the student's form tutor, head of year, or a senior member of staff. They will be able to take action, and may decide to place the student on 'report'. It is important to keep a written record of significant difficulties – your school should have procedures regarding the reporting of incidents.

Around school

Managing behaviour in class is only one part of the picture. For a school to be truly on top of the situation discipline needs to be maintained around the premises: in the corridors, in the halls, at the gates. If most of your day is spent in your classroom you may have little to do with the outside world; but if, in the event of one of those rare trips between your departmental corridor and the staffroom, you should come across a rowdy mob of students 'bunking' their lessons, it helps to feel prepared. Relocating students who are in the wrong place at the wrong time can be an annoying and relentless business. Schools that are efficient about behaviour management may have a network of staff that routinely comb the corridors and round up stragglers. But if you have stumbled across a hidden gang in a faraway nook it may be down to you to escort them to a 'better place'. Here is some advice for dealing with those unwelcome little corridor encounters:

- Unless you are in an 'emergency' type of hurry, do *not* pass the issue by. Even if you are not going to deal with it yourself, raise the awareness of the person that is. Your reputation for addressing behaviour around school will enhance your reputation in the classroom.

- Approaching up-to-no-good students can be unnerving; the risk of receiving a mouthful of abuse is high, a bit of cheek at the very least. Students may be in a rebellious frame of mind, away from the structured classroom setting, and keen to show off to one another. Counter any youthful arrogance by approaching the situation in a stern but calm way: 'This corridor should always be empty during lesson time. You need to get to class immediately.'

- If you have dealings with a student you do not recognize, pinning down their identity is important, in case of the need to chase up the matter. Ask for their name, their year group and the name of their tutor, but be aware that they may try to falsify these answers – pay attention to the distinguishing features of their appearance. Alternatively, catch them on a camera phone . . . though you may need to investigate the legality of this.

- Empty drama studios and gym halls seem to be a magnet for students who want to do inappropriate things: smoking behind the stage curtains, using the crash-mats for 'romantic' interludes . . . it all happens. If you are unfortunate enough to be teaching your class in one of these vicinities your priority will be to turf out the squatters. If they refuse to leave or persistently bug you, then send a trusted member of the class for senior staff back-up. These individuals are not members of your class and therefore strictly are not your problem, but if allowed to linger they may *become* your problem.

- Monitoring the manner and attitude of students around school is a whole-staff issue. If everyone picks up on the niggling problems: running, jostling and shouting in the corridors, impoliteness, aggression and overexcitement at break times, littering, inappropriate language, etc., behaviour expectations will be consistently reinforced and, therefore, more likely to be respected.

General disruption

The majority of problematic behaviour you will encounter in your classroom is likely to be of the low-level kind. Not particularly dramatic but extremely irritating, low-level behaviours can drain your energy and if allowed to continue unchecked may evolve into something more destructive. In short, deal with low-level behaviour. The types of activity I am referring to here could include:

- calling out across the classroom
- talking among one another while the teacher is addressing the whole class
- getting out of seats at inappropriate times
- too much collective classroom noise
- making silly, attention-seeking noises
- giving inappropriate responses to teacher questions
- 'mucking around'
- work avoidance
- lack of basic courtesy
- hindering other students
- cheeky or impertinent remarks
- fidgeting
- unnecessary non-verbal noise (e.g. scraping chairs, tapping stationery)
- infringing class/school rules (e.g. inappropriate dress, eating in class, using mobile phones)
- non-directed swearing (i.e. not *at* anybody)
- verbal banter between students.

These types of behaviour can be commonplace in the classroom, but controlling them can be fairly straightforward if you make a consistent effort. Try to develop and refine some correspondingly low-level strategies that do not involve shouting, screaming and stamping your feet in hysterical fashion; for example:

- *Outline expectations from the start*: Before your teaching begins, take a moment to refresh your students' memories and recap on classroom expectations. Be positive – 'I'm looking forward to a calm, enjoyable lesson today. We've got lots to do, so remember, it is very important that we make an effort to listen carefully, remain in our seats, and raise our hands if we want to speak.'

- *Know their names*: It is so much easier to reclaim student attention when you can be more specific than 'Oi, you!'
- *Use humour*: A quick wit will enable you to make your point while retaining your 'human' side. There is always a place in my heart for sarcasm! Be careful not to over-rely on it however – your students may stop taking you seriously. And never make remarks that are cruel or 'personal'.
- *Refer to the rules*: remind the student of the relevant rule they should be respecting, or better still get them to remind you: 'What is our rule about chewing gum?' Once your students are familiar with the rules you may wish to abbreviate them, for example: 'Eyes, hands, to work please' representing 'Stop turning round to pinch that other boy, and get on with your own work'.
- *Non-verbal signals*: Folding your arms and looking sternly bored while waiting for class attention is often enough to get an echo of 'shh' going. Use your facial expressions and physical proximity (get close to the problem) to make it clear to students that you have seen what they are up to and expect it to stop.
- *Verbal warnings*: Try to give a warning before issuing an outright sanction, giving the students the chance to take responsibility for their own actions. Be firm and direct: 'You need to get your work finished. I want you to stop chatting and concentrate – that's your first warning.' A second warning should involve a consequence of some kind: 'If you cannot concentrate on your work now, you will have to make up the time during break – that's your final warning.'
- *Be explicit*: Be clear and specific about what it is your students are doing wrong, but also refer to what you would *like* them to be doing. Doing this will help to clarify your expectations and lead them towards the positive.
- *Set reasonable consequences*: Detention after school (any more than 20 minutes and parents will have to be informed), catching up on work during lunch or break, a note in their planner, loss of points/merits, loss of privileges, a phone call/letter home (for more serious or repeated problems), verbal or written apologies, referral to another member of staff.
- *Visual warnings*: Use a white board in place of your precious voice when trying to get students settled. You could quietly list

the names of students who are needing to check their behaviour, or you could use a points system: draw a map of the class tables on the board, and then place a mark on each table if they become too noisy – five marks leads to a ten-minute detention.

- *Redirect*: If a student is struggling to maintain concentration or stay out of difficulty they may benefit from a change of seat or involvement in a different activity. Explain that this is not a punishment, but a way of helping them to avoid getting into trouble.

- *Positive reinforcement*: Focus your attention on the ones that are getting it right – 'Well done to the students on this side of the room – I can see that you are ready to listen. Thank you.' Not only does this reward the students who are fulfilling your expectations, but it also provides a massive hint to those who are straggling.

- '*See me after class*': The words that send a fearful chill down the spine of every student (if only!). Use this option when time is of the essence, or when you do not want to lose your teaching flow. Make sure you remember to see it through, or you will risk negating the perceived threat.

Challenging behaviour

Tackling low-level disruption effectively will define your strength as a manager of classroom behaviour, and encourage students to toe the line – but there will, of course, be some exceptions. For various reasons some individuals find it very hard to conform to boundaries, no matter how clear those boundaries are. It is important to be prepared for behaviour that challenges the limits of your expectations, so the following suggestions deal specifically with this issue. (For more detailed advice and ideas look out for another of my books, *Managing Very Challenging Behaviour*.)

First, I wish to outline some of the reasons *why* students engage in more extreme difficult behaviour (understanding is an important step towards developing successful strategies):

- diagnosed/undiagnosed conditions: for example, attention deficit disorder (ADD/ADHD), learning disorders, language and communication disorders;

- underlying emotional issues: depression, low self-esteem, fear, anxiety, trauma, anger, bereavement and loss;
- high self-esteem combined with a lack of socially acceptable values or consideration for others, leading to arrogant, defiant, self-centred behaviour;
- peer influence and social insecurity: the need to present themselves as the 'leader of the pack', or to impress others by complying with misbehaviour;
- academic insecurity: leading to work avoidance and behaviour that distracts from their perceived failings;
- unstable home environment: lack of boundaries, lack of nurture, inconsistent parenting, deprivation, parental lack of value for education;
- frustration: not being able to understand (e.g. English as an Additional Language), or be understood (feeling as if no one values or listens to them);
- living up to a label: constantly being told you are this, that or the other can lead to a negative self-image;
- lack of self-control: student has not developed the skills to contain their own aggression, excitement or energy;
- excessive need for personal control: student feels the need to be in control of every situation and reacts badly to minor confrontation or challenge;
- circumstantial: difficulties in a previous lesson, falling out with friends, tension at home, bullying, etc;
- overexcitement: after break times, or due to incidents in or out of school (e.g. fights, fun events, weather);
- dietary issues: junk food (need I say more?);
- attention seeking: either from other students or adults (if they cannot get it in a positive way, they may seek it in a negative one);
- boredom: lesson is failing to reach student, because it is too difficult, too easy, or just plain dull;
- problems with teacher: inconsistent or unfair behaviour management, disrespectful manner towards students, signs of apathy or lack of interest (e.g. regularly turning up late, failing to set purposeful work), failing to do anything about classroom behaviour, power seeking or confrontational approach to students.

I have spent much of my career working with BESD: students with emotional, social and behavioural difficulties. I have learned that difficult behaviour (even the irritating, petty things) can always be explained in some way. This does not make it acceptable, or excusable – but it hopefully sheds some light on the way forward. We will have more success with challenging young people if we endeavour to empathize with their circumstances, provide them with supportive stability (setting firm boundaries, remaining calm, being consistent), and help them to develop the capacity to manage their own feelings and behaviours. There is also a great need to address the origins of these problems, but these are often issues that are beyond the teacher's remit, as one frustrated colleague once implied: 'I am *not* a social worker!'

Working with vulnerable, volatile individuals is intense and demanding work. It is something I chose to do, but I sympathize with those who have not made that choice yet still find themselves contending with extremely challenging behaviour within their mainstream classes. These are the days of 'inclusive' education. While many schools are embracing the inclusive ethos, the one area they are struggling to cope with is – you've guessed it – challenging behaviour. I have also, however, encountered many schools that are thriving within the inclusive ideal. They tend to have strong whole-school behaviour policies, and staff that are committed to overcoming the practical hurdles of inclusion, as well as embracing the 'vision'.

As a teacher in an inclusive environment the issue of challenging behaviour may be very real to you. For all the opinions that are held by the government, the media and the public, *you* are the one who actually has to contend with it. I cannot offer you a magic wand, but I can provide some tried-and-tested advice on how to handle difficult situations. These may include:

- verbal abuse
- offensive remarks
- threatening behaviour
- physical aggression
- damage to property or the environment
- refusal to cooperate
- wilful and persistent disturbance
- absconding or running away.

Although tactical ignoring can be an effective way of dealing with low-level problems, the above types of behaviour should not be ignored. Stop whatever else you are doing and focus your attention on the student(s) in question. Your initial aim should be to de-escalate the problem – in other words, do not rise to confrontation. Get their attention (move calmly towards them and/or firmly repeat their name) and endeavour to stabilize the situation before getting down to the 'telling off'/consequences part. You may be tempted to scream, shout back, and project your 'power', but this is likely to make it worse. Focus on calm assertiveness:

1. Do not rant on for ages – keep your commands simple and clear: 'Pushing each other is unacceptable in this classroom. You need to stop right now.' If necessary, raise your voice and repeat these commands until the student takes notice, but do not lose your temper, as this will be counterproductive.
2. If a student is angry or upset, try to identify with their feelings: 'I understand that you are feeling very annoyed, but if you calm down I can help you sort the problem out.' Offering to be an ally, rather than an enemy, will avoid power struggles.
3. If a student is rude or insubordinate towards you, be matter of fact about it: 'That sort of comment is not acceptable here, you know that.' And if they persist: 'I'm not interested in having an argument with you, but I will be happy to talk about the problem with you when you are able to talk about it calmly with me.'

When both you and the student are calm enough (a period of time-out or with another teacher may ease this process) the behaviour itself will need to be addressed. Talk to the student on a 1:1 basis, either after class or away from prying ears. Listen to their version of events, and then outline why the behaviour is unacceptable and what the consequences will be. These consequences could involve apologies, detention, a conversation with parents or referral to a senior member of staff. Opt for the latter if you feel the problem requires further attention.

For serious breaches of conduct (including persistent refusal to follow your instructions) or dangerous behaviour, additional staff back-up should be sought, and the student removed from the class – many schools have a 'call' system, or a policy whereby students can be sent to another teacher. Avoid using this procedure for minor incidents, however. If you want your students to take your behaviour management seriously, they need to see you dealing with it.

If you are significantly shaken by an incident you may wish to have temporary respite from the classroom. There is no shame in this, and most staff would be more than happy to step in and protect your welfare. Finally, remember to write up an account of the incident as soon as you are able – the information you pass on may be critical to the outcome.

3 Managing the classroom

Organization

Keeping control of the space you work in can sometimes be as difficult as keeping control of the children that work in it. Classrooms are busy places: the potential for mess is everywhere. Mess can be demoralizing – for you and your students – so it is helpful to get on top of it before it gets on top of you.

A certain level of mess will be dealt with day to day, by ancillary staff. But the real problem is what I call 'organizational' mess: what happens when there are not enough homes for items to go to – when the paper cupboard (and all its thoughtfully recycled scraps) starts to regurgitate, when the sunflowers fall from popularity and are left to rot on the window sills, when your table top becomes your filing cabinet, and when neatly formed groups of desks sneak apart and block all known access to the other side of the room.

So you are confident that your entire term's planning is in there, along with Class 5's science books, the departmental stapler, and most of the staff room coffee mugs. And you would definitely wash up last week's art materials . . . if you could just get to the sink. Sounds like a clear-out is due:

- Get students involved – helping them to develop a sense of pride and ownership over their learning space.
- Chuck out anything that is broken, useless, or smells peculiar.
- Organize/reorganize files for your paperwork and establish one accessible place to keep them.
- Develop the habit of filing things as soon as you produce/receive them. You may consider having files for: current planning, long-term planning, worksheet masters and

photocopy resources, an SEN file, a tutorial file, an assessment file.

- Create spaces or 'zones' for different classroom activities: art, science, reading, ICT, literacy, numeracy, etc.
- Organize classroom stationery into trays, draws or desk tidies, and encourage students to put things back appropriately.
- Collect up all stray stationery and get someone to test the pens, felts, etc. – chuck out/recycle the broken stuff.
- Laminate posters and signs: preserving their lifespan.
- Label draws, cupboards and other storage, helping you and your students to know where to put, and then subsequently find, things.
- Attach cardboard folder wallets to the wall by your desk – one for each class or subject, and use these to store relevant pieces of paper (planning, work sheets, last week's homework, etc.).
- Encourage students to assist in maintaining organization: give regular reminders, assign certain duties or responsibilities, and factor 'tidy-up' time into your lessons.
- If necessary have one cupboard space where miscellaneous items and old paperwork can be 'dumped', while you decide whether they are worth keeping or not.

Safety

Solid expectations regarding safe conduct in the classroom are important for a number of reasons. First, they are obviously necessary to protect individuals from causing harm to themselves or others. Secondly, they encourage more orderly movement and activity within the room, which, in itself, makes for a calmer environment. Lastly, they are useful to draw upon in times of discipline, enabling you to separate your personal opinion from the necessary rules: 'What you have done has put yourself and your friends in danger, and I'm afraid, regardless of how sorry you tell me you are, that has to be treated very seriously.'

The expectations you put in place will vary according to the subject(s) you teach and the spaces you teach in. For general guidance, consult your staff/departmental handbooks, and make sure you know the correct procedure for that important event in the school day/week/term: the fire alarm. Some additional tips:

- Set out clear rules for health and safety in the classroom. These may need to be temporarily redefined for certain types of activity. Follow through with clear consequences for anyone caught abusing these rules.
- Provide visual information as well as verbal, for example using diagrams to illustrate how to cut away from your hands when using sharp tools. Visual material may have a stronger impact on some students.
- Outline health and safety issues *before* giving out relevant equipment – otherwise there will always be someone who is not paying attention to you because they are too busy misusing said equipment!
- Use brightly coloured gaffer tape to mark the safest route through the classroom/lab, and to demarcate areas that should not be entered without supervision.
- Use lockable storage for potentially dangerous items such as craft knives or hazardous materials. Ensure that you monitor the number of items given out and collected in, thereby avoiding stray equipment falling into inappropriate hands.
- When teaching in 'open' environments, such as halls or studios, emphasize rules for appropriate movement and physical interaction before, or as soon as your students enter the room – open spaces seem to automatically increase youth excitability.

Inspiration

Making your room organized and safe is only part of the process – you also need to make it a place that your students like coming to. A room that is bursting with colour, information and eye-catching visual stimulus is welcoming and invigorating. The easiest way to achieve this is by developing classroom displays:

- Organize themed boards (relevant to whatever topics/ subjects are being covered, or perhaps by year group).
- Change displays frequently – nothing is less inspiring than sun-faded, dog-eared work by students who left the school five years ago.

- Combine factual information, images, sound bites and titles, with examples of student work. Avoid large amounts of small printed text, as it is unlikely this will ever be read closely.
- Unify the display, by using only two or three colours of backing paper (one for the background, and contrasting colours for backing work), but do not feel everything has to be set out in organized rows – be adventurous!
- Take pride in displaying student work, encouraging them to take pride in themselves. Thoughtful mounting can make the most of the least.
- Incorporate work from all levels of ability, not just the most able, but avoid putting up work that you know students have made little effort with, it sends out the wrong message.
- Involve your students in the process – taking the pressure off you, and allowing them to have some ownership over the appearance of their classroom.
- Reinforce learning, by setting up a relevant display at the start of a new topic. Keep some parts of it blank and you can motivate students to produce display-worthy work to go up there.
- Alternatively, set up your display just *before* you start a new topic or subject, and give them a tantalizing glimpse of what is to come – they'll spend half-term excitedly chatting about it – won't they?
- Make displays interactive – incorporate the class computer(s), or include 3-dimensional models and artefacts. Students could even design a class website within which to display their work.
- Keep the area surrounding where you 'stand and deliver' your teaching relatively simple – you want their eyes and attention to focus on you.

4 Being part of school life

Sharing an ethos

Beyond the front-line task of teaching, there is an entire school to be part of. Not all schools are the same. Some may focus on moral and spiritual well-being, some may favour academic competitiveness and have a hard line on discipline. Some schools may adhere to a particular belief system, provide single-sex education, or promote excellence in a certain subject area. Also, schools are increasingly adopting an inclusive ethos, providing mainstream 'education for all'.

Prior to joining a school it is important to pay attention to its aims and intentions – know what you are getting involved with! If you are a staunch atheist, with a hatred of religious indoctrination, do you really belong in a convent school? Teacher/school fit can make a huge difference to your enjoyment of the job. I have known many colleagues who have had their attitudes to work transformed by a change of environment – some have escaped the 'horrors' of inner city secondary schools for peace and tranquillity in the private sector. Others have fled from the 'stifling formality' of the latter to find vibrant excitement within urban comprehensives in special measures.

Being comfortable with your school's atmosphere and ethos is not only beneficial to your happiness, it is vital to the machinery of the school itself. Schools that are consistent in their promotion of certain aims and values are more likely to achieve what they set out to do – the message is everywhere. A 'whole-school' approach, in which staff are united in the way they do things, has had proven success, not least in the area of behaviour management. Consistency is vital. If you personally are not bothered about maintaining strict uniform codes and enforcing a no-baseball-caps-in-class rule that is up to you, but you will be at odds in a school that is. Yes, you may win popularity among the students; but you will also be undermining the work and effort of many other hard-working members of staff.

Inclusion

As inclusive education is on the agenda of schools throughout the country (and world), I feel it is important to clarify exactly what this means. In short, it represents the principle that every child has a right to be educated, and that this should happen within the local school community – thereby reducing barriers to learning and participation in school life, combating discriminatory attitudes and helping to build an inclusive society. What this means on the ground level is that mainstream schools have adapted or are adapting their services to accommodate young people with a range of needs and issues. SEN is a term that seems to be synonymous with inclusion, but in fact inclusion encompasses many other areas:

- minority ethnic and faith groups
- travellers, asylum seekers and refugees
- students who need support to learn English as an Additional Language (EAL)
- gifted and talented students
- gender issues
- children looked after by the local authority
- sick children and young carers
- children from families under stress
- pregnant schoolgirls and teenage mothers
- students who are 'at risk' of disaffection and exclusion.

While it is difficult to deny the positive value of inclusive ideology, it is not difficult to admit that it represents a considerable challenge to schools and their staff. Effective inclusion requires commitment. Schools may have to adapt their approach to almost every aspect of the education experience: the building, the curriculum, the attitudes and values of staff and students, teaching support, funding mechanisms, policies, staff training, learning resources, partnerships with parents and other professionals.

Schools that successfully embrace the inclusive ethos tend to have a positive view of the difficulties they are presented with. They regard challenge as a set of hurdles to jump, rather than problems to complain about. They recognize that compromises have to be made in order to accommodate the needs of everyone, but that meeting those needs has a positive impact on the wider community, and enriches the experience of staff and students alike. Being part of a school that is working in this way can be exciting and fulfilling: positive attitudes and keen determination abound. But for schools that are struggling, inclusive policy can seem like one enormous headache – and this includes establishments that have the best of intentions but are suffering through lack of funding, resources, experience or leadership, and/or are simply overwhelmed by the number of 'included' students they have to manage.

SEN

The term 'special educational needs' represents a variety of issues that can affect an individual's access to learning and education. These are broadly defined by the SEN Code of Practice as:

- communication and interaction
- cognition and learning
- emotional, social and behavioural development
- sensory and/or physical.

Although special schools still exist, many SEN students are now educated in mainstream environments. Inclusive schools may cater for students with various different needs, or provide specialist provision within a particular area. There is also likely to be a team of staff dedicated to SEN (including the SEN coordinator (SENCO), behaviour support teachers, learning support teachers, and an army of support assistants (LSAs)). These are the staff who are in the 'know', and can provide you with information and advice regarding the needs of individual students. Additionally, there may be external staff entering your realm from time to time: educational psychologists, educational welfare officers (EWOs), speech and language therapists, staff from special schools or behaviour support services, to name but a few. They will be carrying out observations and assessments and, if you are lucky, sharing their expertise.

As a class teacher you will be expected to contribute to the identification and assessment of students with SEN, as well as making provision for them to engage appropriately with your lessons. Any opportunity to undertake training in this area should be grabbed with both hands – many teachers complain of feeling poorly equipped to deal with different needs. Working with SEN has the potential to be a very interesting and rewarding aspect of the teaching role, but is sometimes maligned by the pressure to rattle through the curriculum and improve overall class achievement. The two things can, of course, happily coexist, but this takes skill and experience. If your first few years in an inclusive school feel slightly desperate, never fear – your skin will thicken over time.

Pastoral care

Anticipating my NQT year in a busy secondary school, I was annoyed to discover I had been given a form group to tutor – as if I didn't have enough to think about. By the end of that year my attitude had changed entirely: being a form tutor was one of the most enjoyable aspects of the school day, and certainly one of the most rewarding. It allowed me to explore and develop the way I relate to my students, and helped me to establish my classroom identity – without the burden of 'If I can't get them to do more work, it will be my fault they fail their GCSEs'!

Pastoral care allows you to get to know and appreciate members of your form group as characters and personalities, beyond league table statistics. One of the key aspects of the role is regard for student welfare and emotional well-being. This can be as simple as providing a listening ear after a falling out with friends, or as complex as monitoring a child protection issue. Unless you have a particularly anti-social manner (and sometimes, *especially* if you have an anti-social manner) some student somewhere will try to get in touch with your humanity. There are several different ways in which you may find yourself providing personal and social guidance for your students:

- *Providing reassurance at the start of the year.* If you have a first-year group, you will need to shepherd them through their early weeks, ensuring that they are familiar with their timetables, finding their way around, and getting to grips with the school day. You may also need to offer additional support to anxious individuals – look out for those who seem withdrawn or nervous.

- *Dealing with disclosures and child protection issues*: From time to time students may approach you with personal problems that are of a serious or sensitive nature. Having someone share information with you that is perhaps disturbing or upsetting can be an unnerving experience, but remember, if the student has chosen to share it with you, it is likely that they trust you. You will need to respond in a way that is calm, respectful and ethical. Disclosures will need to be passed on to the school's designated child protection officer (CPO), and it is therefore important to forewarn the student that this is the case. It is also important to remember – for your own protection – that you should avoid being alone with an individual student behind a closed door.
- *Looking out for their well-being*: Having daily contact with a group of students, either as a class teacher or form tutor, can give you clear insight into their ups and downs and will help you to identify problems. Look out for changes in mood, changes in appearance (for example, sudden weight loss or gain), excessive tiredness, social isolation or withdrawal, involvement in arguments, unauthorized absence and odd behaviour. If you have general concerns about an individual, discreetly ask them if everything is OK and offer your time, should they wish to talk. If you suspect the issues are serious you should seek the support of more experienced staff and/or the CPO.
- *Addressing bullying*: If members of your form group are involved with bullying (either as victims or perpetrators) you may play a vital role in terms of addressing and monitoring the situation, as well as providing emotional support and nurturing their self-esteem. You may be one of the first to notice a bullying issue, given that you have regular contact with the same group of students. It is important that you know what policies and procedures your school has in place to help you to deal with the problem.
- *Providing a listening ear*: Sometimes your students may just want to offload their worries and will come to you for a shoulder to cry on. If you happen to have a sympathetic ear you may

find that the troubled souls begin to line up outside your door: some with genuine problems, some just wanting a wee bit of attention – before you know it you are the lower school agony aunt! Do not feel you have to be available all of the time. Some schools now have professional counsellors/student advisers to whom you can redirect the needy.

- *Defending their honour.* You will probably have teachers coming to you as a form tutor to complain about difficult students, and you will undoubtedly have students in your form coming to you and complaining about difficult teachers! Sometimes the form tutor's position is a precarious one: balancing the attitudes and opinions of staff with the attitudes and opinions of students. It is worth remembering that – on both sides – these attitudes and opinions can sometimes be unjustified.

Beyond the 'care' aspect of pastoral work there is a neat list of responsibilities that comes attached to the role of form tutor:

- accurate and orderly maintenance of the register
- checking and signing student diaries/planners
- inducting first-year/new students
- issuing letters and notices
- pursuing reliable (i.e. authentic) absence notes
- collecting reply slips/trip money/contact information
- monitoring the progress of students who are 'on report'
- chasing up other teachers' 'complaints' or disciplinary matters
- correlating and proofreading subject reports, as well as making form tutor comments
- communicating with parents and attending parents' evenings
- organizing and performing form group assemblies, as required
- reporting to head of year/assistant head of year, and attending year group/tutorial meetings
- getting involved/supporting year group activities: charity fundraising events, sports tournaments, trips, etc.

Duties

Standing in the icy winter air, minus gloves and scarf, children gnawing at your feet and pulling on your favourite jumper, while you wait impatiently for the moment you can ring that bell . . . too late for you though, your cup-a-soup has long since cooled. Ah, the joys of break duty.

The additional duties that befall the average teacher are generally not all that popular. The type and number of tasks you will be expected to undertake will vary from school to school, but the three common ones are break duty, cover, and exam invigilation (NQTs are given a lighter load). They are easy to complain about: break duty = irritating, cover = time wasting, invigilation = Boring (with a capital B). However, as the oil that keeps the school cogs whirring, they are perhaps a necessary evil.

Conscientious management will try to organize the break duty rota so that teachers are not 'sandwiching' it into their busiest day, but it is not always possible to be this flexible. If you are unhappy with the timing of a duty you may be able to find someone who is happy to swap with you. But you will soon learn that it is not just the mere existence or the timing of the duty that bothers teachers so much, but the *location*. In primary schools this generally means outside – which is fine in the summer, not so fine in the winter; and in secondary schools, this could be any number of places . . .

The ICT corridor is generally quite a nice one, usually occupied by a quiet group of 'Dungeons and Dragons' fans. The stairwell next to the boys' toilets is not too pleasant – it stinks, and there is always a mutant group of 13-year-olds putting you off your morning doughnut as they attempt to 'get off' with one another. The worst of the lot, however, is the one that involves parading the school perimeters to check for escapees – often resulting in confrontation with lippy 15-year-olds, and then endless amounts of chasing up.

Cover or the 'art of taking over an absent teacher's lesson' is also hard to get excited about. Having intended a productive afternoon of marking and planning, you glance at the cover notice board and realize you are down for bottom set double drama – roll your eyes and deeply sigh. Your only consolation is that watching this bunch try to perform Shakespeare might be the funniest thing you will ever see.

And as for invigilation – there is no way to glamorize it. It is *unbelievably* boring. You cannot talk, eat, read, get some marking done, or even doodle amusing cartoons of odd-looking students. You simply have to walk up and down rows and rows of desks, listening to the clock tick, and handing out sharp pencils. Adding insult to injury, the weather outside is likely to be glorious.

Meetings

Well-run, efficient and purposeful meetings are an essential opportunity to share and gather information. Unstructured overlong affairs, full of irrelevant issues and too many people who like the sound of their own voice, are highly frustrating. Inevitably you will come across both during your working life: your survival kit is a notebook and pen. In the former, they will help you to keep track of useful details. In the latter, they enable you to plan your weekly shop/list your top ten songs beginning with the letter 'P'/draw up a will. Expect to be involved with a number of different meetings relating to different areas of school life:

- *Whole-staff meetings*: These may be a combination of daily/regular 'briefings', usually before the school day begins, and longer, more formal sessions. Briefings aid the day-to-day running of the school, and are an opportunity to exchange information, give reminders, and ensure that everyone is aware of any changes, new students, visitors or events. Some managers also view them as an opportunity to give staff a 'pep' talk. The more formal version may occur on a termly/half-termly basis and will be organized well in advance. This sort of meeting may continue for an hour or more, and will cover whole-school matters, such as development plans and inspections.
- *Departmental/curriculum meetings*: These are regular meetings (once a fortnight or month), in which subject-related information is discussed. They will usually take place after school, or at a time when everyone is available, and are an opportunity to review matters such as syllabus requirements, assessment issues, exam moderation, homework policies, trips, projects and schemes of work. In the primary school, meetings may be dedicated to single subjects, such as science, and are a useful opportunity to pick up new ideas.

- *Year group pastoral team meetings*: These meetings are an opportunity for form tutors from a particular year group to get together and discuss pastoral issues along with their head of year and deputies. This may involve planning trips or activity weeks, organizing competitions and reward systems, looking at strategies for improving behaviour, and dealing with individual students.
- *NQT/induction meetings*: As part of your induction, or as an NQT, you may be expected to attend regular sessions with other new teachers in the school. The programme of meetings will be put together by those in charge of induction, and should cover a variety of topics to do with general school life and teaching. If well organized, these can be a welcome support and source of information during that daunting first year, and will give you the opportunity to meet other new staff within the school.

Extra-curricular activities

For some, having responsibility for extra-curricular activities is a reason to go to school each day. For others, it is a no-go area. The activities on offer can be invaluable to the students who take part in them, enriching the school experience and encouraging individual aspirations. If you can spare some time (without overloading yourself with additional work), getting involved with a club or activity can be a rewarding and fun experience. Some schools may expect you to participate automatically. If you are looking for something to get involved with, here are some suggestions:

- *Subject-based clubs*: Most departments will have some kind of club: art, drama, modern foreign languages, science, computers, etc. Even if it is not your own teaching subject it is unlikely that an offer of assistance will be turned down.
- *Sports teams*: Usually the domain of the PE staff, and may involve early Saturday mornings! If you have a particular sporting interest or skill (ex-aerobics instructor, synchronized swimmer, pool champion or ballroom dancer) there may be scope for a club of your own?

- *Music*: Most schools have active orchestras, choirs and maybe smaller bands, and some will combine the talents of staff and students alike, giving you the opportunity to dust down that ageing clarinet and relive your childhood fantasy of being a 'musician'. If you are an enthusiast, and vaguely cool, there may be opportunities to help promote the interests and talents of musical students . . . schools are riddled with aspiring indie bands, Metalheadz and MC crews!

- *Drama*: Theatre productions benefit from assistance in a number of ways. If you do not fancy directing, producing, or even treading the boards, you may consider getting involved with lighting, costumes, set design, promotion or make-up. Drama clubs are often fun and lively occasions, and a chance to see the stand-up comedians/Shakespearian actors/soap stars of the future – and you spotted their talent before they were famous!

- *Communication*: School councils, newsletters and debating societies are a refreshing chance to see young people channelling their opinions, and exercising their vocal chords in a productive way. Organizing activities such as a school magazine can be quite demanding on time, but may add an exciting new dimension to your work satisfaction.

- *Start your own*: If you have some fantastic hobby or talent, why keep it to yourself? Surely the whole world could do with decorative napkin-folding lessons? Or how about a chess club, film club, environmental awareness club, 'fashion' club, or disco dancing . . . the opportunities are endless, and you might even get some funding.

The benefits of getting involved with extra-curricular activities are plentiful. You and your students will see each other in a new light. You will interact with a wider group of individuals, which will be beneficial to your reputation around school, not to mention your reputation among senior staff: 'That new teacher in the science department – what a *live wire*!' Make sure that you can manage the time commitment, however; and always adhere to health and safety regulations. If you are running your own club you will need to organize an appropriate location and additional staff supervision.

INSET

Teaching is a job that will continually evolve, whether you want it to or not. Opportunities to widen your skills will help you to evolve with it: take advantage of INSET (otherwise known as in-service training). If you are fortunate, your school will have a handsome training budget and a keen interest in developing the staff, enabling you to access more than just the standard whole-school training days (which are usually dominated by gripes about the quality of the training day lunch, and how we would all rather be clearing our store cupboards than listening to some has-been droning on about pedagogies).

You may be recommended, or even required, to attend certain courses, but you will also be encouraged to reflect on your own interests and aspirations. Think about areas of school life that interest you (pastoral, SEN, management, etc.), or aspects of your subject that you would like to develop (using ICT, for example). You may also choose to look at ways of developing specific classroom skills: either a weakness that you would like to improve, or a strength you feel you could develop expertise in (differentiation, behaviour management, providing for different learning styles, etc.). If you do some research within your borough (many will have their own education training centres) or perhaps through the Internet, you will probably find something to suit your needs. There is nothing to stop you putting forward a request for a course that you feel may help you, as long as the demands are reasonable – that three-week wine-tasting course in Tuscany is perhaps not the way forward.

Courses vary in length and intensity. Some may be academic (leading to a postgraduate qualification), which is great for the CV but could be demanding on your personal time: background reading and essay writing. Others will be shorter (one or two days), or perhaps an evening a week. After attending a course you may be expected to share what you have learned with other members of staff, so remember to keep a copy of the handouts.

Part Two

What does Training Involve?

Although there are now several different pathways to qualified teacher status (BEd, PGCE, GTP (Graduate Teacher Programme)), they all revolve around one central idea: teaching *practice*. In other words, putting you into a classroom and letting you get on with it. Well, perhaps it is not quite as brutal as that, but if you were expecting to doze in a cosy lecture theatre for the course duration you will be in for a shock. And so you should be! The majority of trainee teachers I have encountered agree that, despite the initial terror, being in the classroom and simply getting on with it is the fastest and most effective way to learn.

Depending on your training programme, you will have one or more full/part-time school placements, which will be combined with a series of college sessions and lectures. In addition, you will have meetings with course mentors, who will give you 1:1 or small group feedback and support on various different aspects of your progress. You will have essays and coursework to produce, some of them useful, some of them perhaps not so useful; and basic skills tests, which need to be passed before you can be awarded QTS (qualified teacher status). Oh, and did I mention observations? Nothing to worry about – just a few experienced professionals coming into your lessons and judging your every move.

Expect to work hard, expect to feel tired most of the time, expect to feel antagonistic towards certain aspects of your teacher training college (many students do) and expect to have moments of utter despair (usually when a coursework deadline is approaching). But other than that . . .

5 Making the most of your placement

Working on the basics

During your training you may come across the type of trainee who takes to teaching like a duck to water. Fresh out of university and sickeningly confident, they appear to have been doing it all their lives, bouncing around the classroom with immaculate lesson plans and permanent smiles. Well, good for them. But while they are pro-grammed to be teaching *machines*, we – the majority – have been doing exciting things with our lives, like . . . hmm . . . like, staying up all night to watch the snooker and . . . other things . . . oh well.

If anything, however, teacher training is a chance to make mis-takes, to muddle through and be unsure of what is happening. Never be ashamed of struggling. The struggle is what helps you to learn. You are joining a profession that is difficult to totally master, because it is always evolving. Any experienced teacher will tell you that they regularly face new experiences and new opportunities to do things differently. In your training year and, in fact, your first few years, you may find yourself staring down from the tip of a very large iceberg!

The moral of this message is: do not try to do or be too much during your training year. Before worrying about outstanding exam results and perfect behaviour, concentrate on getting the basics right:

- feeling/appearing confident in the classroom
- developing a calm and assertive teaching 'voice'
- exploring ways of engaging student attention
- giving clear and direct instructions
- practising positive communication
- providing simple, well-structured lessons
- establishing a sense of lesson pace and timing

- establishing and reinforcing basic boundaries of behaviour
- developing good habits of paperwork organization
- familiarizing yourself with the curriculum basics
- familiarizing yourself with school routines and procedures
- finding easy solutions to common problems (for example, students who finish work too quickly, children who refuse to take part in activities, etc.).

And if some of your lessons go wrong – so what, you're a novice!

Learning from others

A well-structured teaching placement will provide ample opportunities for you to observe other teachers in action. Although you may prefer to be getting on with the job yourself, take advantage of this now, because it may be harder to find such opportunities after your training. Observation enables you to see what needs to be done from an objective position, and can provide plenty of hints and ideas for you to try in your own classroom. If it feels demoralizing to watch another teacher effortlessly manage a class that you really struggle with, remind yourself that they have years of experience ahead of yours. Try to understand what it is they are doing that is making the difference, and then look at ways of introducing this into your own teaching. And if, on the other hand, you think you could do a lot better . . . be quietly confident.

When observing other teachers it can be helpful to focus on specific things, for example how they meet and greet the class, how they get them settled or how they deal with disruptions. Having a focus will help you get the most from the experience, and can be tailored towards your needs and concerns. If it is possible to speak to the teacher before and/or after the lesson, this will give you both the opportunity to discuss any queries and consolidate ideas. Try to see a number of teachers, from different subjects and year groups. It is likely that you will see much variation in style and approach to classroom management: some of it may appeal to you, and some of it may not, but it all contributes to the learning curve.

Opportunities to learn are not just restricted to the classroom. Watch the way other teachers behave around school, in assemblies, or when dealing with difficulties in the playground. Conversations in the staffroom with fellow trainees or other teachers may give you the chance to swap insights and gain new ideas – if there is one thing I have discovered, it is that teachers love to talk about teaching.

Asking for help

Certain requirements have been put in place to ensure that you receive adequate support from your placement school, including assigning you a mentor who will be your key link. If you feel appropriate support is not forthcoming do not be afraid to raise your concerns. Schools are busy places, and your particular agenda may (often unintentionally) not always receive priority attention. If the situation does not improve, despite your requests, you may need to discuss the matter with your college. Schools are paid to receive trainee students, and therefore have a duty to provide for you.

Even with the most supportive of schools/mentors, there may be certain issues that you continue to struggle with. Do not suffer needlessly: if you have a problem, ask for advice. If your mentor cannot give you the answers they may be able to direct you towards someone who can. If you come across a teacher who has an incredibly well-organized planning file, or a remarkable behaviour management technique, ask them what their secret is. They will enjoy the ego massage, and you might learn something useful. Better still, find someone who has an in-depth understanding of educational theory and get them to write your essays for you . . . no!

Being reflective

Perhaps the most important skill you can develop while in training is the ability to be reflective about your teaching practice. Reflection encourages you to learn from your efforts, and will help you to understand the ways and wonders of the classroom environment. Being reflective is about looking back over your daily experiences and analysing the outcomes. It is not about berating yourself for making mistakes, but looking for reasons why they came to be and how they could be avoided. No experience is wasted in reflective teaching practice (even total disaster), for each one provides the material from which you can renew your understanding of what does and does not work in the classroom.

Effective reflection requires you to be somewhat objective – and honest – about yourself. This is not always easy to do, so it may be helpful to ask yourself a few key questions to prompt your responses. Clarify in your mind the situation you are concerned with (for example, an argument with a difficult student who refused to cooperate with you), and then consider the following:

1. When were you first aware of the problem?
2. What did you do to intervene?
3. How did the student(s) react to this intervention?
4. How did you react to their reaction?

These questions can be repeated as you consider each stage of the unfolding drama. It may be helpful to write your answers down. Be as objective as you can, although you should also try to reflect on how the situation made you feel and whether your feelings affected your interventions. Once you have established the key information, analyse it: look at links between your feelings and interventions and the outcomes. If you had reacted differently, do you think the outcome would have been different?

Team teaching

Team teaching involves two teachers working alongside one another with one group of students, sharing the effort and responsibility. It is sometimes used in teacher training to aid the initiation of the novice. Being paired with an experienced teacher provides plenty of opportunity to watch and learn, while still giving you the chance to be 'hands on'. Some schools are beginning to use it in a more general way (where staff resources are good) to provide more intensive support for classes.

The benefits of team teaching are obvious: students receive more teacher supervision; teachers are able to divide the workload and focus on particular areas (e.g. behaviour, low ability), knowing that the rest of the class is less likely to be neglected. Ultimately this can lead to improved results and less stress. However, team teaching success is not automatically guaranteed. There are a few things that need to be considered in order to ensure an effective partnership is created.

Not all teachers are comfortable about sharing their space with a fellow practitioner, particularly not one who is young and enthusiastic. Even very experienced teachers can be insecure about their classroom methods. If you, as a trainee, have been paired with such an individual, tread carefully. Be willing to take the lead from them initially, and assert yourself gradually. If they give you feedback and advice that comes in the form of outright criticism, take it with a pinch of salt: they might be feeling just a little bit threatened.

A more successful team teaching partnership will require some initial strategic planning. It is helpful to meet beforehand to clarify how the lesson will proceed, and to look at aims and objectives. You may agree to have one person lead the lesson, from whom the other takes their nod of assistance; or you may choose to share roles and responsibilities between you, for example one person dealing with behaviour while the other focuses on learning objectives.

Observations

Lesson observations are something that many teachers dread, but during your training you will have ample opportunity to get over the worry. Expect to be observed on a regular basis, by both your school and college mentors. Some of these observations will be informal. You may not be expected to prepare anything special and your mentor may be keeping a general eye on your progress, providing hints and tips along the way. Others will be formal: the basis for an in-depth written evaluation of your lesson, which you will get to discuss after the observation. Although this kind of observation can be daunting, try to view it positively. With any luck you will have a mentor who makes you feel encouraged and reassured, and gives you sound, constructive feedback.

It is not particularly pleasant having someone scrutinize your actions, but remind yourself that they are not looking to catch you out. They are looking for ways to guide you, to identify your strengths and give you suggestions for further improvement. They will not be expecting perfection. If you are honest with yourself about your strengths and weaknesses, and are willing to confront these issues in a positive way you may find observation and feedback very useful to your development.

Observations are, of course, a way for college tutors to assess your progress and ultimately your pass or failure of the course – but do not panic. If you have made a conscientious effort to nurture the skills that lead to classroom success, this will be evident in your final assessment whether you realize it or not – those destined for failure tend to be picked out earlier rather than later. For formal observations follow these guidelines and all will be well:

- *Be prepared*: You should be given prior notice, allowing you to organize your lesson and resources well in advance and thereby avoid last-minute stress.
- *Showcase your abilities*: It looks good if you can deliver a lesson that falls within the context of an ongoing scheme of work, but it may be prudent to manipulate the lesson content slightly in order to make the most of the opportunity. Lessons where you introduce ideas or activities give you more scope to show off than simply having your students 'carry on' with what they were doing last week.
- *Provide a lesson plan*: Your mentor will expect to see that you are able to teach to a plan, and that your planning is appropriate to the age and ability of your students. Give them a copy before you start, but remember to have a copy available for yourself, in case you need prompting – this is not the time to go wandering off on interesting intellectual tangents!
- *Stick with what you know*: Try to incorporate a mixture of activities and approaches, but avoid doing anything entirely new or unexpected. If you are too adventurous you risk 'throwing' your students or, indeed, yourself. The more you can anticipate the response of the class the easier it will be.
- *Keep an eye on the time*: Your mentor will be just as interested in how you end the lesson as in how you begin. Make sure that you have a plenary planned, and that you allow enough time for this to take place. Likewise, keep an eye on the pace throughout the lesson, ensuring you have time to adequately address the activities you have planned for.
- *If the students do terrible things* . . . Remember, you are not being judged on how your students act (that is up to them), you are being judged on how you deal with their actions. If a crisis occurs just follow the appropriate procedures (e.g. seeking

other adult support, sending the student to another teacher) and remain calm – these things happen and your tutors will understand that.

- *Relax and think positively*: Often the extra bit of effort put into the preparation and delivery of an observed lesson results in an efficient and successful teaching experience – enjoy it! And remember, genuine enthusiasm for your subject and your students may be more endearing to your mentors than flawless delivery.

6 Making the most of college

Lectures and college sessions

As part of your training you will be expected to attend lectures and/or college-based sessions, for one or more days a week. These sessions are intended to give you instructional and theoretical grounding regarding a range of teaching or subject-related issues. You should be given a programme of lectures/sessions at the start of the course, along with reading lists and course handbooks.

The usefulness of college-based activity is often a matter of debate for the student teacher population: it seems many favour the immediate reality of being in the classroom over lecture notes. Others recognize the value of underpinning classroom experience with taught sessions and theoretical direction. College attendance provides opportunities to make regular contact with fellow students, which can be good for morale, plus, let us not forget, a day in college can also be a welcome respite from the pressures of school!

It is likely that your college-based training will involve a combination of lectures, practical workshops, group discussions and 1:1 tutorials. Hopefully your tutors have done all they can to ensure that the sessions they provide are dynamic, inspirational and relevant, and that a broad range of important topics is covered. An inevitable frustration with one-year training courses such as PGCE or GTP is limited time: big issues such as behaviour management, inclusion, differentiation and assessment are often allocated only one or two sessions, when in reality they may take a whole career to get to grips with. Unfortunately it is these very issues that cause the most stress for inexperienced student teachers.

Coursework

As if you do not have enough work to do in the classroom, you will also be required to produce several pieces of written coursework during your training. These may include formal essays on aspects of education theory and practice, maintaining a journal of your experiences, written critiques of your own lessons or schemes of work and, last but not least, a portfolio of 'evidence' to account for what you have learned. Some of these tasks will be ongoing, such as a journal or portfolio, and others will be one-offs.

Combined with lesson preparation and planning, the workload can feel heavy, so it is important to pace it well. People differ in the way they like to get their work done, but the important thing is to find out early what works for you: one big effort or little and often? Generally I would suggest that if you are worried about staying on top of everything, you should resist the temptation to leave coursework to the last minute (especially ongoing tasks that can be difficult to catch up on). If you can develop organized habits and set aside a regular time each day/week to concentrate on journals, portfolios and researching essay topics, you should be able to make it in a relatively stress-free manner.

If it has been some time since you last had to write an extended academic piece of work, you may be approaching your coursework in trepidation. Here are a few tips to make the experience a little easier:

- *Choose the right title*: If you have to choose an essay title or research project, pick one that combines personal interest with 'research-ability'. Obscure topics can be interesting, but difficult to get information on, making them more time consuming. Avoid topics that seem instantly boring to you, as this may impede your motivation – if you can select something that may actually be useful to your teaching so much the better. Make sure you fully understand what the title is expecting from you.
- *Be well prepared*: Try to begin your research well in advance, allowing you time to source a variety of texts. If you can be broad in your approach (using examples of several different types of evidence: books, journals, articles, and the Internet),

you will be able to present a more balanced argument. Essays that have been well researched tend to be a more impressive read.

- *Gather information together*: Save time and energy by spending a few focused hours in the library going through books and other textual material and copying out/photocopying relevant sections or quotes – remembering to make a thorough note of the page number, date, title and author of your source. You will then have this evidence directly to hand when you begin writing your first draft.

- *Answer the question*: You may be full of ideas and inspiration, but you need to make sure your writing has focus. Construct the content of your essay around the specifics of the title question, including the introduction and conclusion. Each time you write a new paragraph, or even a sentence, refer back to your title question and check that it is truly relevant.

- *Back up your argument with evidence*: Try to include relevant quotes and textual references for each key point that you make. This will help to clarify and convince the reader that you know what you are talking about, and show that you have considered other opinions. Remember to pay attention to the context of your quotes: do they represent current thinking, or are they out of date?

- *Avoid too much personal opinion*: If you choose to express your own viewpoint, make it clear to the reader that it is specifically *your* viewpoint, otherwise your essay may seem as if it is full of sweeping generalizations and godlike judgements. A way to avoid too much of the 'personal' is to do your background research and incorporate evidence of this into your writing (see above).

- *Ask someone else to check your work well in advance*: Too many essays lose valuable marks because of sloppy writing and grammar. If you are not confident about your own writing abilities, ask someone who is to correct your work and give you an honest opinion about its quality. Avoid rushing at this stage – if you have made the effort to write it, you should at least take the time to ensure that it is well presented.

Part Three

Coping with Your First Job

The first few years of a teaching career can be challenging and intense. The learning curve is steep and the pressure to get it right may feel immense. As soon as you are left standing alone in front of a class an ominous sense of responsibility washes over you. If your scheme of work backfires, if you cannot control the students, if you cannot get them to produce a scrap (and I mean scrap) of work – it may seem as if the success or failure of an entire generation rests upon your shoulders.

Pupils, parents, and sometimes other staff, will expect you to deliver the necessary classroom skills *before* you have had a chance to discover them for yourself – and do not think you can escape that burden, as one colleague regretfully did, by asking your students to go easy on your inexperience: a red rag to a bull. The only way through is with graft and determination. You will need stamina, enthusiasm, and a willingness to accept (and learn from) failure. You will also need patience, quick thinking, and the ability to multi-task like never before.

On the plus side, conquering the teaching game is undoubtedly achievable, and when it happens it is hugely gratifying: suddenly students are acknowledging you politely in the corridors, they write the date in their books before you ask them to, several of them hang around after class to tell you how interesting your lessons are (and this time, you know they are not just trying to find out what you first name is!). Once you have a grip on the basic requirements of the job the rest of your career is liberated and will become all the more rewarding for the fact that you can now take chances, develop areas of interest, and enjoy the spoils of confidence.

In the meantime . . .

7 Finding one

Applications

Most schools will expect you to fill in a standard application form, but some (usually only independent schools) may request a curriculum vitae/application letter. In either case, the trickiest part is likely to be the 'personal statement' section of information: an opportunity for you to outline in your own words why you would be suitable for the job, what you have to offer, etc. A mini self-advertisement, which is fine if you are brimming with self-assurance, bewildering if you are not. The good news is that, as you progress through your career, you will find the process gets easier – more experience gives you more to say about yourself, as well as more confidence.

The rest of the information you will be asked to give is likely to be standard: dates and simple descriptions of previous jobs, courses, education, qualifications, and personal details such as National Insurance and DfES numbers. It is worth keeping a master copy of all of this information on one sheet of paper – it is a pain to have to dig it out each time you apply for a new job. Here are some other hints on fuss-free job applications:

- *Give them what they want*: Adapt your personal statement to ensure that it reflects what employers are looking for. Necessary attributes and experience will usually be clarified in the person specification/job description. Go through the list and think of concrete ways in which you fit the criteria – responsibilities in your previous job, experiences you have had, personal qualities you possess, training you have undertaken. Employers will go for evidence and examples over lists of adjectives to describe how great you are.

- *Tailor to the job*: If you are applying for similar positions in different schools, always check the person specification and adapt your application accordingly. Although jobs may be similar at first glance, different schools may have different requirements and criteria. Showing how you fit their specific expectations suggests that you are seriously interested and puts you in a higher league.
- *Big yourself up – truthfully*: Job applications are a chance for you to promote yourself and take some pride in your achievements: think positive. But be realistic. If you helped to develop your school's anti-bullying policy, do highlight this as an achievement, but be careful not to imply that you single-handedly wrote and delivered it (it may sound impressive on paper, but if it is not true you will get caught out in the end).
- *Check it through*: Or ask someone to check it for you. If the form can be word-processed you will avoid worries about making mistakes on the original. If your handwriting is dreadful (as mine is!), I would suggest word-processing anyway. Send it off in good time, but always keep a photocopy for yourself – an aid to your interview preparation.

Interviews

So the big day has arrived. You are sweating it out in the front seat of your car, waiting for a 'reasonably' early time to approach reception, and hoping no one from the school is watching as you fluster through your notes and nervously adjust your hair. Your chance to shine . . . or be crushed? Arrive on time. Be prepared. Smile and be friendly. Dress well. Stay calm. All good advice, but what happens when your mind goes blank, your mouth goes dry and the interview panel stare at you with menacing expectation? What you really need to know is this:

- *Remain in command of yourself*: It is perfectly acceptable to pause, to request time to gather your thoughts, to ask for the meaning of a question to be clarified, or to add further comments to a previous question that you feel you did not answer adequately. Interviewers would much rather hear considered, thoughtful responses than slick, over-rehearsed patter. Think of it as a conversation about you and your teaching, but remember to keep your responses as concise as possible.

- *Think positive, feel positive*: If you feel good about yourself and your work you may find you can actually enjoy the interview experience – after all, there is a captive audience wanting to hear all about you and your achievements. Viewing the interview as an opportunity, rather than a challenge, will help you to relax and do yourself justice.
- *Be open*: If you are asked about something you are not sure of, give an honest response. For example, if you are asked about child protection issues and have had no training in that area, offer a common-sense answer (i.e., what you 'think' you should do) and then explain that although you have had limited experience of this issue, it is something you are keen to learn about. Showing that you are willing and motivated is better than trying to show that you know it all (especially if you don't!).
- *Preparation, preparation, preparation*: It cannot guarantee a successful interview, but it certainly helps. You can prepare in several ways:
  - Knowing what to expect of the visit (practical tasks, teaching a class, a tour of the school, panel interviews).
  - Working out how to get to the school in advance.
  - Anticipating some key issues to talk about (e.g., inclusion, differentiation, behaviour and attendance, assessment, equal opportunities).
  - Practising responses to common questions (for example, why do you want this job?).
  - Reflecting on some good examples of classroom triumphs and challenges to support your answers.
  - Ensuring arrangements are made with your current school regarding cover and time off.
- *Be ready to ask questions of your own*: They will ask if you have any questions, so it is helpful to have some in mind – but choose carefully. The topic of money is generally best avoided. Enquire about things that matter to you such as training opportunities, plans to develop the department, or the ways in which senior management support their staff – it will not hurt to put them on the spot for a moment!

The one for you?

Hooray, you have been offered the job – only problem is, you don't want it! Doing some research before making your applications will help you to make decisions further down the line and avoid wasting time on jobs you do not really want. Once you have the name of a school you can find information about it on the Internet: the school website, Ofsted reports, news articles, LEA information. If the school is local you may be able to get the low-down through word of mouth.

Most head teachers will invite potential applicants to visit their empire before interview date. If you can get there, I would strongly recommend this. It gives you an opportunity to have a good nose round before making further commitment. Of course you may encounter a fair amount of 'gloss', but you should still be able to gather a reasonable sense of the place if you read between the lines. What is the building like? How much care is put into displays? How friendly are the staff? How do students relate to one another? How do staff relate to the students? How organized is the reception (often a telltale sign)? What are the facilities like?

Try, if you can, to stick around and witness a break time, and make sure you get the chance to visit the department in question. You should also be given the opportunity to have a brief chat with relevant staff members, if they are not too busy. Ask questions and, if possible, gently interrogate a couple of students – their opinions are likely to be quite revealing.

8 Getting prepared

Holiday planning

No, not planning your summer holiday. 'Doing' planning in your summer holiday. I must confess I have never been one of those teachers. I am happy to work hard during term time, but my holidays are my own. I shudder when I hear colleagues exchanging comments about how many days of half-term (often most of them) are spent with noses dipped in their planning files, and I wonder whether it is because they are mad, or because I am simply lazy! I know I am not lazy, so I figure I must be doing something right.

Initially, planning can be time consuming. It takes experience to establish a format that is both efficient and trustworthy (in other words, enables you to deliver), so you may feel the need to put in a few extra hours while you can. The holidays provide breathing space to do this, but avoid going overboard. Restrict your planning time to a particular week, or couple of days, therefore making it less likely to encroach on the time you should be relaxing. If it helps, go into school or to a local library where you can work in peace, while separating school from home. And at the end of the day, reward your efforts with a lovely glass of wine.

One of the most helpful methods of planning is to work within the aforementioned long/medium/short-term framework:

- *long term:* half-termly topic/module titles for the whole year, which can be filled in on one easily accessible timetable;
- *medium term:* your schemes of work, corresponding to the aforementioned module titles, and providing a week-by-week breakdown of learning objectives;
- *short term:* daily lesson breakdowns, providing more detailed information about activities, resources and learning outcomes.

During the holidays it is advisable to focus on long- and medium-term planning (although bear in mind that some departments will do this collaboratively), which will set you up for the rest of the year. Develop some short-term plans for the first few weeks of teaching, but beyond this you may find an awful lot changes – suddenly your pupils are not as bright as you thought, or they start complaining that they have already covered that topic. Too much detailed planning too far in advance can be a waste of energy.

Coping with new-job anxiety

It is not uncommon for trainee teachers to be offered positions in the school where they have trained. This has many advantages: you will know the school and its routines, you will understand how your department works, and you will have some familiarity with staff and students. However, if this opportunity is not available to you, or you feel you would benefit from a fresh start, you will have to go through the process of getting to know a new environment – which can bring as much anxiety as it does excitement.

Hopefully your new employers will do what they can to prepare you for the start of term, ensuring that you know times, dates and first-day schedules. It is possible you will be given the opportunity to spend one or more days at the school prior to joining. This is a great chance to get to know staff, find out about resources/curriculum issues, and feel a bit more established before the 'big day' comes along.

If you have a whole summer holiday ahead of you, try to enjoy your freedom while you can. You may be tempted to plan an entire year's teaching, or fret about behaviour management techniques. You may find it difficult to relax as the end of summer draws near – a feeling of impending doom. But *do* relax – keep some perspective. Get yourself prepared for the first term/half-term, read a few teaching books if it helps, but no more. Use the time to have fun, and return to school refreshed.

Psyching yourself up

Two days to go. You have chosen your outfit, worked out your route (making time allowances for traffic), and organized your bag. Now all you have to do is wait. Excited? Nervous? Miserable? Returning to the classroom after a long, and hopefully glorious, summer can feel like a wrench. All that time to get used to waking up without the alarm clock, doing as you please when you please . . . suddenly snatched away from you and forcing you into a mercilessly hectic timetable with a 7am start! Fear not. After a week you may find the return to routine strangely comforting, and soon enough you will forget you ever had a holiday at all.

There are a few ways in which you can help yourself mentally and physically prepare for the long-haul term ahead of you. First, get yourself organized a few days in advance, avoiding a last-minute panic and allowing you to enjoy the final moments of holiday time. It may be helpful to touch base with colleagues or course friends, to wish them well and remind yourself that you are not in this alone.

Try to get as much rest as you can, but consider retraining yourself to get up earlier during the last week of the holidays (unless, of course, you have young children, in which case you have probably been getting up early throughout!). This will encourage your body clock gradually to adjust to early starts, and avoid one big nasty shock. Some people have trouble sleeping for one or two days before a significant event or change. If this is affecting you, make a special effort to relax and deal with your school worries during the daytime. Talk to family and friends and get concerns out of your system, so that you do not find yourself churning them over in the middle of the night.

I imagine I am not alone in this, but throughout my first few years of teaching the end of the holidays always brought a feeling of dread that I would not be able to stand up convincingly in front of a class, as if I had entirely forgotten how to teach. This anxiety would plague me right up until I actually walked through the school gates, then – as if by magic – I would automatically slip into teacher mode and feel completely unbothered by it all. If you experience something similar, remind yourself that all your teaching knowledge and expertise is still in there, it has simply been lying dormant for a few weeks (and a good thing too!). It will reappear when you need it, I promise.

9 Making a positive first impression

The first day

The first day of the autumn term is often an INSET day, giving staff a chance to reorient themselves and get organized. If it is your first day at a new school you may have a whole set of questions and concerns of your own. Here are some tips to help you make the most of the time:

- *Expect to feel awkward:* Walking into a large room full of people who already know each other, who are chatting amicably and exchanging banter, can be quite intimidating. But you will not be overlooked forever – in fact, it will only be a matter of moments before you are asked to stand up in front of the entire room and give a three-minute introductory speech about yourself.
- *Find your way around:* In a big school there may be areas that you never need to go to, but on your first day you will at least need to find out how to get between the basics: your department, the hall(s), the staffroom, the offices, the photocopier, the canteen, the staff toilets and, of course, the exit. Hopefully you will be supplied with a map, but if you can get someone to walk you around, so much the better.
- *Get acquainted with your room:* After the meetings (and there may be a few!), you may have a little preparation time on your hands. If you have your own classroom spend some time getting a feel for the space – check the arrangement of the desks and test out equipment (windows, blinds, computers, interactive white boards, etc.). It is unlikely that you will have time to start putting up elaborate displays, but you may want to personalize the space with a few posters or a welcome sign.

- *Grab for resources:* Many people will try to give you things on your first day: timetables, class lists, staff ID, planners, IEPs, handbooks – when actually all you want is some white board markers and a coffee mug! Do, however, get what you need in order to be prepared for your first lessons. Find out where stationery, including textbooks and display materials, are available from; and remember to chase up important details such as keys, computer log-ins and photocopier PINs.

The first lesson

Actually, there may be a few 'first' lessons throughout the first week. Each time you encounter a new class you will have to go through the process of introducing and establishing yourself. First lessons are an important time, because they give the class the opportunity to size you up. If you want to make a positive first impression it is worth putting a bit of thought into the way you present yourself and the activities you provide. If there is one bit of advice that I would give to new teachers, it is this: project an air of confidence and authority whenever you enter a classroom or greet your students – and then continue to do this for the rest of your teaching career. Even if the confidence is not genuine (teaching is much akin to acting), a projection of boldness will grab your students' attention and get them thinking, 'Aha, this is one of those teachers who gets us to sit up and listen.'

First lesson jitters are often unfounded – these early encounters are usually the easiest. For a start, you may find most of the session is taken up with administrative tasks: issuing exercise/textbooks, computer passwords, etc. Your lesson content will be fairly straightforward, outlining course content/learning aims for the forthcoming term. You may also have a captive audience. Students tend to be quite timid at the start of term (according to staffroom legend: 'the honeymoon period'), and will listen and cooperate with minimal effort from you. Do not be fooled – in a fortnight it may be very different! Make sure you consistently bed down your expectations *before* they are challenged.

Some teachers use the first lesson to clarify class rules and procedures, with discussion and tasks based around appropriate conduct. This has the obvious benefit of establishing expectations right from the start, and ensures that students understand you are the kind of teacher who sets boundaries. Inviting the class to contribute their own ideas and opinions will encourage them to have some ownership over classroom expectations and, therefore, a greater sense of responsibility. Activities could include:

- group discussion and brainstorming acceptable/unacceptable behaviour;
- compiling a want/do not want list, from which to establish several key rules;
- teacher provides class rule 'contracts' for students to discuss and then sign;
- group activity: each group is given a class rule, about which to plan a poster/role-play/debate, and then present to the rest of the class;
- teacher-led rant about behaviour expectations – not particularly inspiring, but a clear way of making your point;
- rehearsing exemplary behaviour and routine expectations, such as how to line up or how to ask for help;
- work the seating plan – arranging students as *you* please will establish your control over what happens within the space.

One disadvantage of focusing on rules is that it may be happening with every teacher in every lesson: students will get bored of the dogma. If you really want to grab their attention consider doing something subject related, which will get them excited about the term ahead: a dynamic demonstration or interesting activity. Something I have learned when teaching students with behavioural difficulties is that they like to 'do stuff' – long periods of teacher talk can lead to problems. Getting your class engaged with an exciting practical activity or display could be a way of winning over some of your more disruptive students.

Developing a classroom persona

As the first term progresses you will gradually find your teaching rhythm. The shape of your week (the busy times/the quiet times) will become more familiar to you, and the true natures of your students will begin to emerge. But as you become more settled it is important not to become complacent: the classic teaching cliché, 'Don't smile till Christmas'! By all means smile, but remember, you are still a relatively unknown entity to your students. If you let your guard down too soon they may decide to take advantage. Make a continual effort to maintain high expectations and assert classroom boundaries, and your reputation will gradually take root. Once your reputation is firmly established it will do much of the work for you.

How you choose to assert these boundaries and expectations is down to your individual approach and personality. Although there are common traits that enhance the process (being calm, consistent, firm, fair and positive), there is still plenty of room for personal teaching style. Teaching style is something that you may think about consciously, or that you may pay no attention to − simply being yourself. However, it is helpful to be able to adapt your persona according to age, need and overall attitude of individual classes. Some groups may require a bit more nurture; others will need a no-nonsense approach.

Laid-back, super-strict, enthusiastic, funny, caring, eccentric, scatty, efficient, sarcastic, grumpy . . . remember that whatever you project will influence the way your students feel about you. If you want them to like you and enjoy coming to your lessons you will need to make them feel welcome and inspired. If you want them to have respect for you, you will need to show respect for them. And if you want them to feel motivated you will need to give them encouragement.

Try not to fall into the trap of being the 'pupils' friend'. It may be tempting when you first begin teaching (especially if you are fairly close in age to some of your students) to try to get them on your side by being easygoing and familiar. This may prove effective in the short term but usually backfires as time moves on, with students deciding that they would rather have 'a laugh' than do any work for you.

If you feel that things have slipped, or that your current classroom approach is not working, it is never too late to turn the situation around. You can re-establish firmer classroom control and/or a more positive attitude to learning, but you will need to accept that you have to change before your students can. Take time to reflect on what is going on and why, then think about ways in which you can improve the experience − if necessary seek advice from a more experienced teacher. A considered effort over several weeks, with plenty of modelling of desired behaviour, will help put you and your class back on the right track. Remember, however, that classroom management is a process: expectations and routines require time to take hold. A common mistake is to give up on a strategy just because it fails to have immediate effect.

Learning the school ropes

During your first term you may feel somewhat bombarded by information or requests for it, as the school works through the process of getting to know the new student/staff intake, and settles itself into the new academic year. Over time you will be able to digest it all, and separate the useful from the pointless. As a new staff member/NQT you should receive some form of induction, which will help you to familiarize yourself with the quirks of your particular school, but if you are not sure, ask.

You will need to get to know, or at least be aware of, certain staff members who may be of use to you: heads of year, special needs staff, departmental/curriculum leaders, classroom assistants, subject technicians, senior staff, CPOs, union reps, learning mentors, behaviour support teachers, caretakers, and administrative staff. Knowing exactly who to talk to about a specific concern or issue can save you time and worry. If you do not like the thought of bothering busy people with your problems, remind yourself that good schools rely on good teamwork and good communication. Most staff members will be happy to offer support or share advice; if not, then they are in the wrong kind of job.

You will, of course, need to get a grip of your basic timetable, but also the when and wherefores of assemblies, meetings, duties and extra-curricular activities. Another thing you will soon discover is that schools tend to thrive on routines and systems: how to request photocopying, what to do if a child has a nosebleed, where to send an irate 13-year-old, what time your class has to line up for lunch. Although some of these will amount to little more than filling in the right form and placing it in the right pigeon-hole, others are the lifeblood of smooth operation within the school. Familiarizing yourself with routines and procedures will help you to streamline your working day.

Survival

Part Four
Valuable Personality Traits

Progressing in your teaching career will allow you to learn new things about yourself, as well as about the job. It may test you in a variety of ways: how strong you are, how organized, how intuitive, how ruthless (!), to suggest but a few. It can be intensive, both physically and emotionally. Of course it can also be extreme fun and very interesting, but do not be surprised if you often feel as though you are being stretched from pillar to post. Students, parents and other staff members will constantly make demands on you, while in the meantime you will have to plan, prepare, mark, assess, review, differentiate . . .

The following part of the book is concerned with the question: what does it take to remain sane in the classroom? The three useful traits I have decided to focus on are commitment, patience and self-confidence. There are indeed many other qualities and attributes that are advantageous in the teaching profession, but these three have helped my colleagues and I through some dark times, and are especially helpful when it comes to coping with the day-to-day rigours of school life.

The importance of being committed to the job stands to reason, but since it is a job – and not necessarily something people do because they really, truly want to – I will be exploring some of the ways in which commitment can be nurtured and maintained. Patience, apart from being a virtue, is a definite asset when working in the classroom: without it you would probably end up wanting to boil your own head. And as for self-confidence, perhaps this is the most important of all. This is an industry in which you will be 'on show' for most of the working day. If you are not comfortable with people looking at you, listening to you and making comments about you, you may find it rather unpleasant.

10 Commitment

Is it what you want?

People choose careers in teaching for many different reasons. Some may enjoy working with young people, others may be passionate about their subject. Some may believe in the fundamental importance of education, others may have been lured by the idea of long holidays, job security (the world always needs teachers), 'golden hellos', being your own boss, escaping from the office environment. Whatever factors lead you into teaching, perhaps you can only truly confirm it is for you after you have done it for a few years. By then the romantic myths will have been dispelled, but you will also have enough experience under your belt to feel confident about what you do.

New entrants can be put off very quickly, finding themselves overwhelmed by issues such as difficult behaviour or workload. If you find yourself wavering, talk to more experienced teachers. Some will complain bitterly, but many will tell you that it gets much easier after the first few years. If you can get over the hurdle of inexperience you may find a rewarding and interesting career awaits you. If, however, you cannot get past the frustration and disillusionment, you may need to think carefully about your commitment.

It is a hard job to do if you do not really want to be doing it. (It is hard enough when you *do* want to be doing it!) If you want to do justice to the profession and the students you will need to commit yourself to providing a high standard of practice, and giving all the energy, organization and enthusiasm that this entails. There is little room for casual effort: a busy classroom is not something a teacher can enter mindlessly – half an hour late, somewhat hung-over, and completely unprepared. Well, OK, so we all have our moments, but generally there is a need to be 'switched on' and ready for the lesson.

If you are not 'in the mood' can you honestly expect your students to be?

When the going gets tough . . .

There is a simple yet wonderful cure for the aches and pains of teaching: a sense of humour. It cannot plan your lessons for you or guarantee good behaviour, but it will help you to cope with the difficult times. Being able to look back and laugh about a chaotic lesson or disastrous incident will relieve pressure and help you to move on. An experiment goes unexpectedly wrong, little Gemma is sick over her SATS papers, Gary calls the school inspector a tramp – sometimes classrooms are unpredictable places, but because of this they are also fun.

Seeing the lighter side of school life is not just about frippery, for many it is a coping mechanism. If we took every little problematic incident seriously, personally or angrily, our nerves would be completely shattered before long. It is no coincidence that staffroom conversations often involve the ridicule of the students: wound-up teachers are letting off steam. From bitchy sarcasm to practical jokes, a sense of humour gives us resilience and reminds us to take pleasure in what we do.

No matter how intense your day becomes you can always find something to smile about, even if it is a smile of pure malice! If a lesson goes wrong, tell yourself you will at least get an amusing anecdote out of it. I have kept friends enthralled for ages with tales from my BESD classroom. They are under the impression that teaching is just one funny event after another and, while they are miserably pushing paper clips around a dusty office, I might just allow them to think that.

Stamina

Although teaching may not be thought of first and foremost as a physical job, it can certainly take it out of you. Unless you are the kind of teacher who stays wedged into your desk from dawn till dusk you will be on your feet for a large proportion of the day. Pay attention to the amount of walking around you do. The length of the classroom is not very far, but the length of the classroom $\times$ 100 starts to add up – no wonder you flake out on the sofa every evening!

It is not just constant movement that can tire teachers out – all that thinking is burning up a surprising amount of energy. Having to be vigilant about behaviour, at the same time as concentrating on what you are saying, at the same time as dealing with questions and demands from students, at the same time as keeping in mind the overall aims of the lesson, is quite a feat. It is something we get used to doing, but it will always be demanding.

In order to keep up with the pace, give what is needed and reduce the risk of wearing yourself out, it is important to take care of your physical and mental health. I am no fitness guru, but here are some common-sense suggestions:

- *Get regular exercise*: No surprises here. Physical exercise (a minimum of three times a week) not only keeps you trim and improves your overall energy levels, but is an amazing stress-buster. Find something you enjoy and it will easily become part of your lifestyle.
- *Eat well*: Lunch breaks can be quickly swallowed up by clubs, activities or chasing people about, but the culture of 'I'm so busy I haven't had time to eat' is, quite frankly, bizarre. Eating is a necessity, not a luxury. On busy days it is even more important that you give your body the fuel it needs. So eat up, give yourself a balanced diet, and in case of emergency stash some supplies in your drawer.
- *Drink regularly*: Dehydration is a destroyer of energy, but how often do you go through a day of constant talking with only a few cups of (dehydrating) coffee to wet your whistle? Keep a bottle of water by your side at all times – if it is good enough for the supermodels it is good enough for teachers.
- *Build relaxation into your week*: Not just putting your feet up with a four-pack and the idiot-box, but proper pampering for your brain. Set aside time to be quiet and reflective: reading, listening to soothing music, having an indulgent bath, or try meditating/yoga.
- *Rest when necessary*: If you are beginning to feel the strain the most important thing you can do is *listen* to your body – it wants a rest. Yes, your school needs you, but if you are ill or

run-down martyrdom will not help you to recover. Having a few days off at the early signs of exhaustion could possibly save you from having to take six weeks off further down the line.

Pacing yourself

Another way to keep on top of classroom commitment is to ensure that you pace your workload in a way that is both productive and manageable. In an environment where there are many things to juggle, within limited time, it is helpful to feel that you have some control over the amount of work you do, and when you do it. Here are some useful tips on time management:

- *Balance your week*: Your timetable will hopefully have a combination of busy and quieter days (NQTs have reduced teaching hours). On the toughest teaching days, try to keep other commitments to a minimum, allowing you to remain focused. On 'easy' days, catch up on planning or tackle those extra responsibilities, such as lunchtime clubs, chasing up parents or organizing displays.
- *Multi-task*: You may sometimes find yourself in unavoidable time-wasting situations: boring meetings, lesson cover, running a detention. This does not have to be 'dead' time if you are always armed with a notebook and pen – they give you the chance to jot down ideas for a new scheme or work, or to start preparing reports.
- *Make the most of non-contact time*: Hopefully your school has a supportive attitude towards providing teaching staff with adequate preparation time, however sometimes it can be hard to get motivated if you have been busy in the classroom. Avoid procrastination and get started straight away. Find a quiet space (not always easy!), make a list of what needs to be done, in priority order, and then simply get on with it – promising yourself that once everything on the list is crossed off you can relax – with a clear conscience.
- *Know your deadlines*: Reports, marking, assessments, and even planning, all have to be produced within certain timeframes. If you find yourself getting in a muddle over what to do by when, design yourself a simple timetable that highlights each of your

deadlines through the year, enabling you to anticipate forth-coming responsibilities. You might also want to note deadline warnings in your diary, a few weeks before they are due.

- *Set yourself boundaries*: If you feel that taking schoolwork home with you is a bad idea (it generally is!), then make sure you do not have to do it. I am far happier getting in early/staying late to catch up on paperwork than finding it pile up on my living room table – the pleasure of driving home knowing I have a whole evening to myself far outweighs being one of the last to leave. If, on the other hand, I have not got work to do, I feel no guilt about escaping from the building as early as possible.

- *Give yourself incentives*: Fifty reports in 48 hours? Promise yourself a treat at the end of it and you may feel more inspired. Well, it works on children.

11 Patience

Coping with a 'lively' environment

Classrooms can be busy places. The busier they are the more stressful they become. Try these techniques for preserving classroom karma:

- *Establish activity areas*: Organizing your room so that different kinds of activity take place in different areas (for example ICT, quiet reading, art/craft, imaginary play corners) will minimize the risk of mess and chaos spreading throughout the room, and allow you to direct students towards activities easily. Although this is mainly aimed at younger students, it can also be helpful in the secondary classroom (ever thought of a 'dictionary corner' or 'algebra avenue'?).

- *Develop non-verbal control techniques*: Having to shout constantly for attention is probably one of the most stress-inducing things you can do. Teach your students to respond to non-verbal signals and you will be able to claim their attention without straining your voice. These signals could be aural, such as a handclap, bell, alarm, or even a brief piece of music. They could also be visual: a message or symbol on the white board, or a raised arm (ask students to copy you by raising their arms, until everyone in the class has responded – this has the added benefit of getting them to remain focused on you while waiting for others).

- *Give them a countdown*: As you wait for your class to get settled, rather then growing impatient and snapping at them, give them a simple countdown. If you incorporate an incentive into this (such as a class point each time they are ready when you reach zero/two points for being ready by the time you reach three), they will be encouraged to speed up.

- *Try using calming techniques*: If the class seems particularly excitable, or you are anticipating a chaotic activity, take a few minutes at the start of the lesson to establish a calm atmosphere. Try playing some soothing music, or lead a group relaxation activity (you will be able to find examples on the Internet). This could involve getting students to close their eyes and concentrate on breathing or sound – there may be giggles at first, but as they get used to it, it may prove very effective.
- *Easy lessons*: If school life is really getting too hectic there is always the video player (or, these days, the DVD player)! Some may view it as a cop-out, but television *can* be educational (Shakespeare adaptations, 1970s science documentaries and favourite episodes of *Time Team* have long held their place in departmental schemes of work). Besides, pressing the play button allows you to tick your 'incorporates ICT' box.
- *Play sleeping lions*: Now that is a cop-out!

Tolerating difficult individuals

For all the students you will deal with in your career, there may be some that you will find hard to get along with. This does not make you a bad teacher, just a human one. Often we feel obliged to value every single little cherub that graces our classroom, but the true fact is that some of them will make themselves unlikeable to us. They may be spiteful, they may be rude, or they may just be really annoying – attributes we would not tolerate from any other work colleague.

Negative feelings towards students are fine, as long as they do not interfere with the classroom experience; in other words, they are confined to your thoughts or perhaps the staffroom. Allowing personal feelings to encroach on your classroom relationships can be very damaging. At the very least, maintain a professional (neutral) relationship, or try developing an empathic approach. Undesirable behaviour or personality traits are often the result of unfortunate circumstances or experiences: the child that picks on others is deeply insecure; the individual who lashes out has learned this behaviour from aggressive parents. We may do better to recognize that an unpleasant remark from a child is a sign of their own discontent rather than something to be taken personally. Here are some thoughts on tolerating and empathizing with difficult students:

- *Separate the undesirable behaviour from the child*: Make it clear that your dislike of what they are doing is not a dislike of them personally (or at least pretend!). Always avoid labelling students: 'You are really annoying me' or 'You are a nasty of piece of work.'

- *Model positive examples*: If a student has recurrent behaviours that frustrate you (such as fidgeting or answering back) show them an acceptable alternative (e.g. sitting on their hands, counting to ten before responding) and give them encouragement – you may be surprised how well they respond to a bit of positive reinforcement.

- *Never take things personally*: Unless you genuinely are a bitch/whore/witch/wanker/dickhead, there is no need to take the insults to heart. Do you really care what a bunch of grotty teenagers thinks? If your students are critical of the things that you do, or the way that you teach, remind yourself not to rise to the bait – they are trying to undermine you, in order to make themselves feel better.

- *Use the rule of respect*: If a student is rude or unpleasant, emphasize the whole-class expectation of respect for one other. Remind them that this rule applies to everyone, and is wanted by everyone. Encourage them to reflect on how they would feel if you were being disrespectful to them.

- *Offload away from the classroom*: If you feel upset, frustrated or fed up there is nothing wrong with a good moan, but be sure to do it away from your students – if a young person can sense your dislike of them the situation will not improve.

- *Ask yourself what they really want*: When a child is aggravating another student, is their intention to cause annoyance or are they trying to get some kind of attention? If a child starts acting up, are they deliberately trying to ruin your lesson, or are they trying to disguise the fact that they cannot cope with the level of work?

- *Look at it from another point of view*: If a student is being difficult, try to imagine yourself in their position, with their life, their environment, their opportunities. Are you surprised?

If learning doesn't go your way . . .

Teaching can sometimes feel like a battle of wills. You want the class to knuckle down and get on with their coursework – you know what is good for them. They would rather doss around and talk about trainers. Trying to get a group of work-shy teenagers to recognize the wonders of Shakespeare, or the significance of the feudal system, can be an immensely frustrating experience. Sometimes simply getting them to listen may be enough of a struggle.

Sit among a group of teachers for long enough and you will discover that certain classes (usually bottom sets) are famed for their ability to frustrate and infuriate – sometimes to the point where the teacher declares they are 'no longer salvageable'. If, like most teachers, you feel duty-bound to have high expectations of student attainment, the problem is exacerbated.

Of course, it is important to have high expectations of every student (if we don't, why should they?), but these expectations make more sense if they are realistic, and if they are regarded in relation to the student's individual strengths and weaknesses. Many of the young people I have worked with have been completely demoralized by their lack of achievement within the formal curriculum. Their intentions are to leave school as early as possible (or earlier, in some cases!), yet they have so much potential in other ways. If only there was more time to nurture their broader skills and interests and give them more individualized support, perhaps they would have developed a different opinion of school?

Part of the problem is the fact that the British education system is riddled with tensions between provision and improvement. On the one hand we are expected to provide 'education for all', on the other we are pressured to produce improving league table results within a rigid curriculum. But as I am not here to gripe about disconnected, knee-jerk government policies, I will give this advice to the teacher who is weary from trying to fit the wrong student into the wrong type of learning experience: find ways of working 'with' the class, not against them. Adjust your expectations to accommodate their needs (this may mean breaking learning objectives down into very small chunks), be imaginative in the way you present information (make an effort to avoid thinking 'Oh it's only them – they won't get it anyway', look for practical, creative approaches), and learn to be flexible (things happen in lower ability classes that would not happen anywhere else!).

Tips for remaining calm under pressure

Picture the scene. It is Ofsted (naturally). There is a storm blowing outside. You have not had time for a lunch break, and this morning you promised your mixed ability 7-year-olds that they could spend the afternoon making clay men (you hate mess). Add to this the fact that your invaluable LSA is off with flu, your curriculum coordinator wants an inventory of the entire PE cupboard by 9am tomorrow, and your cat needs to go the vet. Most of your students are arguing loudly over how much clay they are allowed, one of them is stuffing it down the plughole, and another has put it in his neighbour's hair. 'Miss, can I go to the toilet?' 'Miss, what do I do with this rolling pin?' 'Miss, how much did you pay for your mobile phone?' 'Miss . . . miss?'

Tell them all to ★★★★ OFF!

No, don't. That is not a good idea at all. Instead, try these ideas for keeping calm when you are in the middle of it all:

- *Keep your own voice down*: Shouting will only increase your stress, and the stress of those around you. If you keep your voice low your students will have to listen harder and therefore be quieter.
- *Deal with one issue at a time*: Accept that you cannot do everything at once – some students will just have to wait. If it helps, sit at your desk and ask them to come to you one by one with their query/problem.
- *Stop the class completely*: If noise and energy levels are going too far it may be helpful to get the whole class to stop their activity and spend a minute in silent contemplation, giving you a chance to rest your ears and allowing a sense of calm to be re-established.
- *Get away*: Feel like you need to scream and stamp your feet? Step outside the classroom door for a moment (pretend you have something important to attend to) and mutter expletives under your breath! Then walk back in and smile.

- *Observe your breath*: Breathing slowly and deeply can help invoke feelings of calmness. As you move around the classroom, try to practise this.
- *Imagine feeling cold*: A bit of an odd one, but an ex-colleague used to swear by it. When we are stressed, our bodies tend to feel hotter (sweaty palms, flushed face, muscle tension). Concentrating on a cool sensation may help to counteract this – think ice cubes!

12 Self-confidence

The value of assertiveness

The ability to project an air of confidence will help you to convince your students that you know what you are doing. If you seem at ease in the classroom and certain of your convictions they will have faith in you. This is extremely important when it comes to discipline. If your attempts to tackle problem behaviour are vague or wishy-washy your students will keep testing you. If you are assertive and firm they are more likely to listen up and take notice. Consider these two contrasting examples.

Example A

Teacher: Umm . . . Jackie . . . umm . . . can you please stop doing that?
Jackie: I'm not doing nuffink.
Teacher: Er . . . well, maybe you're not doing it now, but you were doing it a minute ago. No more, OK?
Jackie: Tch . . . I don't know what you're talking about. I wasn't doing anyfink . . . ask Becky. Becky, d'you know what he's going on about?
Becky: She weren't doing nuffink, sir. You're picking on her.
Teacher: Well, someone was making that tapping sound. Who was it?
Jackie: (*turns to the rest of the class*) Just ignore him – he don't know what he's talking about!

Example B

Teacher: The tapping sound that's coming from that corner of the room needs to stop right away . . . Thank you.

As you can see, the first example wastes valuable time on a discussion that need not take place. The teacher is unspecific about what the problem is, opening himself up to a pointless debate. He plays the ball into Jackie's hands by asking, rather than politely telling her, what she is expected to do. His lack of assurance tempts her into mocking him in front of the whole class. Example B is an assertive and direct but perfectly polite command. There is no undue aggression, or singling out of any student – it is uncomplicated and easy to interpret.

Being assertive is not just about what you say, but how you say it. This is perhaps hard to explain without a demonstration, but I would suggest it is about tone and manner. Think of a voice that is calm, assured, confident and 'friendly'. It is not angry or impatient, and it is not necessarily 'shouty'. An assertive voice may not be your normal speaking voice, so it might be helpful to practise on your own or with a friend, someone who can give you a second opinion/laugh at you. Another useful exercise is to take a tape-recording of your teaching and listen for yourself.

Self-esteem

Teachers spend a lot of time talking about the importance of raising the self-esteem of their students. But what of their own self-esteem? Classrooms can be hard places for the fragile ego to survive in. For a start, the job is demanding and unpredictable; it is largely left up to you to discover what does and does not work, and this can be a steep and difficult learning curve. Secondly, although most of your students will be perfectly charming, there are bound to be some who take great delight in pointing out that your tummy looks pregnant/voice is screechy/teeth are crooked; and, of course, those who give you daily reminders that you are not as good as their previous teacher (who gave them sweets and never told them off – of course not).

The teaching profession at large is not famed for its high morale. Both within and outside of the school gates there is the perception that teachers have been poked, prodded and put upon by various corners of society: dogmatic government policies, scheming Ofsted inspectors, abusive students, aggressive parents. And to the non-sympathizers, we are just a bunch of whingers, ever complaining about money (how dare we?).

Beyond what the rest of the world thinks, however, it is important that you are able to take care of your own self-esteem. Know that all teachers (including the smug ones) have bad lessons; that you are not the only one singled out as the butt of student jokes; and that when they say 'I hate you, you evil cow!' they really mean 'Damn, you've got the better of me!'

Learning from mistakes

One way to remain confident about your classroom experience is to view the difficult times positively – as opportunities to learn – rather than feel disappointed with yourself or your students. I spent some time working as an advisory behaviour support teacher, observing and giving strategic advice to teachers and teaching assistants. A recurring problem was staff becoming trapped within ineffective patterns of behaviour management. With limited training and guidance, these teachers felt bewildered as to how to deal with increasing numbers of challenging students. In desperation, they developed their own coping mechanisms, some of which created more problems than they solved: endless shouting, ignoring everything, removing students for minor issues (what next?), impatient and aggressive tone of voice, giving countless warnings with no follow-up, making personal remarks and criticisms.

Some of these teachers found it very difficult to break out of these unhelpful habits. They were too set in their ways, or maybe they had simply lost the will to keep battling. They were very demoralized and had lost confidence in their classroom skills. Avoid falling into this trap by making the most of opportunities to learn, challenge and refresh your practice. Continue to do this throughout your career and you will be able to move with the times. Things will go wrong occasionally: a lesson plan backfires, the class do surprisingly badly in a test, a school trip results in a visit from the police (oops). Moments such as this could lead you to question your actions, and could easily rock your confidence, but if you think carefully about the situation you may realize there is wisdom to be gained. What could you have done differently to help matters? What will you do next time?

Using advice

As well as developing a personal understanding of your classroom practice, you may benefit from what others can tell you. There will be no shortage of people wanting to give you advice – from interfering head teachers to worthy caretakers – but remember, different people have different priorities. What is right for them may not be right for you. The worst bit of advice I ever received was from an ex-colleague suggesting that I should be a bit 'nastier' to my students. Considering he was later given a disciplinary for slamming a child's hand in a doorway, I am somewhat thankful that I never took him up on it!

Other sources of advice and information on teaching and classroom practice include books (such as this one, of course), school handbooks and policies, websites, government guidelines, training courses and now even a dedicated television channel. If you are looking for fresh ideas, something to get you motivated, or perhaps a bit of reassurance before starting a new job, they can be very helpful. However, there is no substitute for the real thing – the only way to develop true confidence in the classroom is through experience.

Part Five
Skills that Will Help You

Teaching is a practical job. Much of your time will be spent 'doing' and, because of this, it helps if you can keep your classroom well organized, think on your feet, and know what to say without hesitation. You may find yourself leaping from one lesson to the next, without opportunity to pause and take a breath. Once a lesson is done, it is done – there is no chance to say, 'Um, I wasn't quite happy with that, I think I'll go back and change it.' This part of the book looks at some of the skills that will help you to keep your classroom, your students and yourself in order: starting with organizational skills and then covering how to be flexible, how to communicate effectively, and lastly, how to manage stress.

13 Organization

Planning and preparing tasks and materials

Do you like to experiment with different types of learning activity, or do you prefer to play safe and stick to a tried-and-tested lesson formula? Whatever approach you choose, it pays to prepare. And when you consider that you may need to accommodate several different levels of ability and a range of learning styles, it pays to prepare *well*. To some people, efficient organization comes naturally. Others may have to work at it. But fortunately, with a bit of self-discipline, it is relatively easy to master. Here are some suggestions from someone who had to learn the hard way:

- *Start early*: If you know what your schemes of work for the whole year are going to be, you can look out for resources along the way. Record useful programmes, make a note of websites, photocopy relevant articles, collect images, 'borrow' worksheets from your friend's school, etc. Useful things can turn up in the unlikeliest of places.
- *Develop systems*: Self-imposed routines can help you to keep track of what you need to do and when. I try to prepare a week ahead of myself, so that when Monday morning comes around I have everything I need for the lessons that week. I usually do planning, resource gathering and marking on set days (depending on my timetable), and organize the information into separate folders for finished and unfinished efforts (although I must confess, I once got confused and tried to fob students off with a half-written worksheet!).
- *Share ideas*: If other teachers have used or are using similar schemes of work, then try sharing activity ideas and resources.

You may need to adapt them slightly to suit your personal teaching style, but why waste time reinventing the wheel?

- *Make resources reusable*: Keep hold of any materials that could be used for other groups: worksheet masters, planning or photocopies. You may also want to take copies (with student permission) of exemplary pieces of work that can be shown to future classes.
- *Become computer savvy*: Life is so much simpler when you know what to do with a laptop. Putting together exciting resources has never been easier: whole-class presentations, attractive worksheets, marking records. If you are one of those people who still claim to be phobic of ICT, get over it – it is not going to disappear!
- *Get students to help*: Set your students a research task in preparation for a new topic. A bit of independent learning is good for them, plus the swotty ones will hopefully come up with long lists of information, which you can use to boost your own resources!

The classroom with the students

Getting yourself organized is one thing, but getting a room full of other people organized is another. Obviously the task becomes easier if you have the aid of a classroom assistant (or two); but since not everyone has that luxury, here are some suggestions to make active classrooms operate smoothly:

- *Encourage peer support*: If students are encouraged to ask their neighbour for assistance they may be less inclined to harass you unnecessarily. Have an 'ask a friend first' policy, in which students try to help each other with minor problems before seeking adult intervention. This is a great way of encouraging independence and peer support, but may need some monitoring to ensure that the right advice is being given.
- *Write out aims/instructions*: It is helpful to make the aims of the lesson explicit from the start. Write them up/display them clearly, and briefly talk through them with the whole class. Not only will this refresh your memory, but it will help establish

your expectations for the lesson and allay student uncertainties. You can do the same for any instructions you issue. If students are given a simple written reference, as well as a verbal one, the information might just get through.

- *Use a seating plan*: If you have control of the seating plan you may be able to make life easier for yourself. Realistically, your options will be limited by the shape, size and style of your room, and the nature of the students themselves (large numbers of poorly socialized individuals can hamper the number of workable combinations!), but do not be afraid to experiment with different desk arrangements: a large horse-shoe (good for whole-class discussion), rows of Vs (less formal than traditional rows), clusters (good for group work, bad for attention-seekers).

- *Develop routines*: Allow students to take responsibility for organizing themselves and their work efficiently by establishing some whole-class routines. Once they are familiar with the routines you will have less need to nag and chase them up. Routines can help in various situations:
  - Entering/exiting the room. Do they stand behind their chairs and wait? Do they line up at the door? One by one, table by table, or in one big clump? Do they wait for adult permission?
  - Tidying up/giving out equipment. Are different students assigned responsibilities? Do they know where to find things? Do they know safety rules and procedures?
  - Issuing homework. Is it set at the start of the lesson (while students are still alert)? Is the handing-in date clear? Have students understood what is required of them? Is a written description provided, as well as a verbal explanation?
  - Collecting homework. Do you collect it at the start of the lesson (students are less able to escape the consequences of failing to deliver)? Do you make a note of who hands in work? Do you have procedures for chasing up those who don't?
  - Frequently used stationery. Is it easily accessible? Do you trust your students to sharpen pencils or borrow rulers without having to ask for permission? (Giving them some autonomy can encourage them to act more responsibly.)

- Organizing work. Is there a place to put unfinished work, which is accessible to students, should they have some time to finish it later? Is there a place to put completed work, ready for marking?

- *Use class helpers*: Younger students often love being given 'jobs' within the class. This not only helps you, but is good for their self-esteem and sense of responsibility. Make sure you are not just indulging the star students – OK, so perhaps they are the most reliable, but the impact of being a 'helper' can be extremely beneficial for more challenging individuals as well.

The classroom without the students

Some of the foundations of a well-run classroom can be laid without the presence of the students, for instance putting out equipment and/or preparing the space for the lessons ahead. Practical subjects or activities can be stressful if they are poorly organized: arguments over equipment, students milling around not knowing what they are supposed to be doing, essential items unavailable at the last minute. As an ex-art and design teacher, I am well aware of the 'potential for chaos' factor that a practical subject presents. Some departments will have technicians, saintly individuals who are responsible for looking after resources and equipment. Otherwise, you will have to do it yourself. Here are some tips:

- *Make a weekly/daily list*: Work out what resources you need for the week/day ahead and, if possible, collect them all up in one go. There is great peace of mind to be gained from knowing you have everything you need; but if resources are sparse you may need to synchronize with other staff members.

- *Organize a resources table*: It can be helpful to have a table/sideboard that is permanently dedicated to weekly lesson resources, divided into separate sections for each day of the week, or by subject/year group. Having things organized in this way will enable you to access what you need quickly and easily.

- *Lay out trays of equipment*: If students require several different items in order to carry out an experiment/activity (such as paintbrushes or test tubes), have trays of each item on a sideboard or table, from which they can help themselves. When equipment is returned, ensure students place items in the correct trays – making it easy to put things away again.

- *Issue equipment yourself*: If you do not like the idea of students getting out of their seats to collect equipment, you could try organizing a tray for each table, containing all the necessary items, which you can then take to them.
- *Keep track of quantities*: It is prudent to keep a count of what goes out and what comes back in – particularly more 'exotic' items such as glue-guns or bulldog clips. It may take up a bit of extra time, but being meticulous about issuing and collecting equipment sends a clear message to the students about how to respect their classroom and its contents.

All of the above suggestions can apply to more straightforward lessons as well. Textbooks, exercise books and photocopies can be organized and given out in a similar way. The overall message: a bit of organization in advance saves time and stress during the actual lessons.

14 Flexibility

Adapting to the mood of the class

Not only are classrooms busy places, they can also be unpredictable. Sometimes circumstances beyond your control will affect the mood or attitude of your students. Perhaps a lunchtime fight has got them overexcited, or an unexpectedly humid day has left them (and you) feeling agitated and tired? The teacher who is able to 'read' the mood of the class, and adapt their teaching style – or even lesson content – to accommodate changing circumstances will be able to make the most out of any given situation. Some common 'mood' problems, and suggestions on how to tackle them, are given in the table.

Coping with last-minute changes

There is nothing more joyful than the words 'careers talk'. You think you are in for a painful afternoon of bottom-set maths but, just as you start to psych yourself up, the head of year waltzes past and informs you they will all be taking part in a 'careers talk' for the rest of the day. Sweet mercy!

Some last-minute changes are welcome, but some, of course, are not. Can you cover for Miss Brittle? The students frightened her away. Can you squeeze a few more into your room? We don't want 'those' individuals to be roaming the corridors while the inspector is here. Can you teach somewhere else today? I need this room for a dance exam. No matter how efficient you are, from time to time your plans will be compromised.

To a certain extent you can prepare yourself for dealing with last-minute changes: keeping a supply of emergency worksheets, or a stock of tried-and-tested 'fall-back' lessons, but essentially you will need to be able to think on your feet. Although frustrating, at least

Mood	Symptoms	Cure
Lethargy	Students seem tired and listless. Lack of enthusiasm or interest in work. Lots of heads on desks. Frequent yawning.	Avoid tasks that are mentally intensive, or repetitive. Try discussion-based activities, group work, or role-play – get them moving about and engaging with one another. Simple stretches or physical movement may help to re-energize them. Do something shocking or unusual to get their attention.
Overexcitement	More chatter and noise than usual. Students seem 'buzzy' and distracted from work. An increase in silly or attention-seeking behaviour.	Be a firm, calming influence over the class – avoid impatience and accept that this may not be the most productive lesson ever. Avoid introducing new ideas or activities that involve interaction and movement. Keep it simple. Get students engaged with individual tasks they have enjoyed in the past – a good opportunity to revise old topics.
Agitation	Students are particularly argumentative, winding each other up and bickering. Preoccupied with getting at one another.	Take time, at the start of the lesson, to give a firm reminder about classroom expectations and, if necessary, address any arguments or disputes. Choose activities that engage the whole class together (group reading, etc.) so that you can keep a tight rein on them.

an unpredictable work environment gives you the chance to use your imagination – next time you march your class to the ICT suite, only to discover it has been double-booked, spare a thought for the poor souls who work in data entry!

Handling unexpected disturbances

If there is one certainty in the teaching profession, it is this: at some point during the term your lessons will be disturbed by fire alarm practice. The fire alarm: saviour of bad teaching moments, destroyer of good ones. Even when the operation runs smoothly recovery from such 'excitement' can be difficult – do not despair if your lesson plan falls by the wayside. Usually you will be given prior warning if a fire alarm drill is due, although if the fire is genuine (or the prankster is willing) it may come as a surprise.

There are other types of disturbance that can have a shock impact on your lesson: fights, injuries, wasp in the room, or 'invasion' from other students. The latter – bored, out-of-lesson troublemakers trying to distract members of *your* class by tapping on the window/pulling faces/opening the door and making cheeky comments – being the most irritating. It is difficult to deal with a student who is strictly not your responsibility. You might prefer to get on with your lesson, but you will also be obliged to 'turn them in', which inevitably requires some effort. You may not know where they are meant to be, what they are meant to be doing, or sometimes, even who they are.

In situations such as this I have found the 'dismissive' approach quite helpful. I focus on my class: encouraging and praising them for ignoring the 'embarrassingly immature behaviour' of the invader (in the spirit of 'laugh *at*, not with'). I then calmly pop my head out of the door and inform the invader that my class are 'really not interested' in whatever he/she is doing so they might as well go back to their own class. I have also, on occasion, invited the invading student into my lesson: 'You're obviously deeply interested in our group, so you can come in and do the work with us.' That tends to get them moving!

If a disturbance is persistent or particularly obnoxious it may be necessary to request the intervention of another member of staff, who will be able to remove the student from the vicinity and deal with them. Likewise, if the disturbance comes in the form of students fighting, further back-up should be called for. With fights, the primary aim should be to separate the brawlers, and this can be difficult or unsafe if there is only one of you to do it. Once separated, the students will need to be led away from one another to a space where they can calm down, before further interventions are made. It is likely that senior staff will then remove the students and deal with the matter – the efficiency with which such situations are addressed will largely depend on the quality of communication and cooperation between staff members.

Thankfully, events such as fights or aggressive attacks are rare, but if they do occur they can leave everyone, including you, feeling shaken or excitable. Allow some time for frazzled nerves to settle before trying to crack on with the lesson. You may want to give students the opportunity to talk about the event and get it out of their systems, or you may prefer to focus on moving on. Perhaps a last-minute change of activity (something more straightforward and calming) may better suit distracted students. Give praise to any individuals who behaved sensibly during the drama, and try to project a calm, in-control state of mind, which will gradually influence the mood of the class.

15 Communication

Verbal communication

It stands to reason that teachers need to be good communicators: it is the essence of good classroom practice. The clarity, tone and manner in which you express yourself, whether in relation to behaviour or to learning, will make or break your classroom career. You have to make yourself worth listening to if you wish to engage student attention. Is your voice clear, or do you mutter into your own shoulders? Do you give concise instructions, or do you ramble on aimlessly? Do you give 'colour' to your speech, or do you talk in a monotone?

Being a dynamic classroom speaker is not something that everyone can do effortlessly, but it is not an impossible skill to learn. Your confidence will increase naturally as you gain experience. The more confidence you have the easier it is to project yourself. You may also wish to enhance your communication skills by working on the following areas:

- *Giving task instructions*: Make them as simple and clear as possible. Give them out in sequence ('First you need to . . ., then . . .'), and if necessary ask students to repeat them briefly back to you, to confirm understanding. Give them the opportunity to ask questions if they are not sure.
- *Developing your use of student questioning*: Asking effective questions will draw your students into the learning process. 'Open' questions encourage exploration of an idea (such as 'What/why/how do you think . . .?'). 'Closed' or 'specific answer' questions can be used to clarify student understanding ('Who thinks this is correct?', 'What year did the Battle of Hastings take place?').

- *Exploring ideas*: Group discussions are a helpful way of sharing ideas and knowledge, but it is up to the teacher to chair the proceedings. Practise ways of getting the whole class involved ('Who agrees with . . .?'). Eliciting expanded contributions from some students may be difficult, but you will need to make sure that discussion is not monopolized by the confident ones.
- *Present the idea*: The easiest way to generate discussion or interest in a topic is to start with a talking point – a question, an object, visual image, extract of writing, interesting fact or demonstration. If this talking point is exciting or surprising, or presented in an imaginative way, students will take notice. For example, start by telling a ridiculous lie ('I won a million pounds last night!'), and when students are dismissive, play on it. Overexaggerate and insist it is true, until they start to look slightly unsure . . . and so begins your lesson on persuasive writing.
- *Summarizing key points*: When giving a lengthy explanation or introducing a new idea it can be helpful to reiterate the key points in a few simple statements. This can be done as the lesson progresses, or as part of the plenary. Alternatively, you could ask your students to summarize for themselves, testing their understanding.
- *'Putting on a show'*: If you can captivate them with exciting delivery (enthusiasm, expression, and a few jokes for good measure) you are halfway there.

Using positive language

Another important aspect of good communication is the use of positive language and phrasing. It is not something that we necessarily do in our ordinary lives, so it may take a bit of conscious practice. Positive language can be very beneficial to the atmosphere of the classroom. It is particularly helpful if you are responsible for students who have reputations for being difficult or uncooperative.

It involves focusing on 'dos' rather than 'don'ts'. If, for example, you are faced with a student who repeatedly swings on his chair, you would choose to say 'Sit still on your chair' as opposed to 'Do not swing on your chair'. The former response is affirmative: it reinforces a desired expectation. The latter does not offer any direction, and may invite challenge from those who are in the habit of defying the word 'no'.

Positive phrasing can be motivational. Emphasize to your students what you *want* them to do, as though you have faith in them. Even if you have had to reprimand an individual, it is always good to end on a positive note: 'You can make up for your earlier behaviour by showing me what you can achieve. I reckon you'll be able to catch up with the others if you work hard.'

Non-verbal communication

Body language can be just as expressive as the voice – simply standing next to a student, with a stern look and folded arms will signal 'I'm waiting!' When trying to convey subject information, gestures and non-verbal communication can be a helpful way of bringing your spiel to life. Use your eyes, your facial expressions and your hands to express emotion, and to emphasize key points. Don't be afraid to exaggerate – the more animated you are the more entertaining you will be.

There are hundreds of little gestures that can be used in the classroom: looking at your watch impatiently (let's get the lesson started), fixing your eyes on a student and shaking your head (stop that!), putting your finger to your lips (quiet now please), giving the thumbs up when things go well (hooray, you have got some brain cells after all!). Some gestures will be consciously adopted; others will be automatic responses. Pay attention to your own body language during a lesson, and see what goes on. You may be quite surprised.

Body language is a way of emphasizing and strengthening a verbal message, therefore the two need to fit together. If you want your students to have the impression that you are not to be messed with, you will need to reinforce this in every way possible. Telling a student off while cowering behind your desk and avoiding eye contact will create mixed signals. Getting on that child's level, looking them square in the eye and physically commanding their attention, will have greater impact.

Not all body language is helpful. Gestures that appear to be menacing or threatening can be very harmful. It is important to be aware of the difference between assertive and aggressive non-verbal communication – the latter will only lead to further confrontation.

Assertive communication involves commanding an individual's attention while retaining a calm but serious facial expression, giving them adequate personal space, using emphatic but 'open' hand gestures (no fists, no pointing) and keeping these gestures close to your own body. In contrast, backing a child against a wall, gnashing your teeth, and angrily waggling a finger in their face is more akin to intimidation.

16 Stress management

Recognizing stress

This section looks at the issue of stress and what you can do about it. I feel it is important to include such information in this book because of the high incidence of stress-related illness and absence from work within the teaching profession. It would not take a genius to work out why teaching is a stressful career: overworked, underpaid, and all that responsibility on our shoulders. Many of us feel very committed to our jobs – feeling guilty if we are not there, or anxious that everything will go wrong without us. We soldier on no matter what, and tend to accept stress as part of the working day.

A certain amount of stress is fine. It plays a role in motivating a person to get things done, and encourages them to make improvements or find solutions. If, however, the stress is relentless, intense and/or excessive, the effects can be detrimental to an individual's emotional and physical health. Knowing how to identify the symptoms of stress-related suffering will help you to combat the damage it can cause:

- excessive tiredness or exhaustion, which never seems to go away
- feelings of anxiety or constant worry (not just about school matters)
- feeling jittery, or shaky
- loss/increase of appetite
- disordered sleep
- stomach upsets
- frequent colds or illness (stress impairs the immune system)
- change in mood (feeling unusually tense, aggressive, short-tempered, sad, tearful, etc.)

- change in physical appearance (weight loss/gain, hair loss, skin problems)
- feelings of panic or hysteria
- nausea, headaches or joint pain
- tension in the face, particularly around the jaw
- a sense of quickening breath and/or a racing heartbeat
- inability to wind down and relax, even at weekends
- intense feelings of dread about returning to work after a break ('Sunday night blues')
- increased alcohol consumption
- negative self-image
- uncharacteristic feelings of animosity towards teaching and students
- breaking down in the classroom, or feeling unable to cope.

If you recognize any of these symptoms in yourself or your colleagues it may be wise to re-evaluate current working circumstances. What is causing the stress? Does it relate to particular situations, students or lessons? A recent promotion? An increase in workload? Relationships with other staff? Or is it a more general feeling? An accumulative effect? Could the origins be internal, i.e. to do with your own personal issues (low self-esteem, internalized anger, unresolved problems, etc.)? It is worth remembering that stress can adversely affect anyone – from trainee teachers to senior managers. It is about personal perception. What bothers one person may not bother another.

Stress tends to be insidious. It creeps up and takes hold while you are too busy being dedicated to the job to acknowledge its existence. The sad reality is that many people do not realize they are suffering the effects of excessive stress until the total meltdown happens. Be self-aware, and try to confront matters as they arise, instead of squashing them back down and hoping they will go away – they won't.

Getting support

Whether you are just beginning to feel the pressure, or have already reached rock bottom, you will benefit from developing a network of support for yourself. Having support, whatever form it takes, will help you to cope, recover and rebuild yourself. The most

important step is to talk to others. People wrongly assume there is
a stigma attached to admitting they are having difficulties coping
with work pressures, but this in itself creates more stress to deal
with. If you open up to a colleague or friend the chances are they
will identify with you, they will be sympathetic – they may have
their own experiences of stress to share with you.

- *Colleagues*: Letting trusted colleagues know you are having
  problems can be invaluable. They can help you out, cheer you
  up, look out for you, and above all, they can *understand* what
  you are up against. Opening up to them may also feel like a
  huge weight has been lifted from your shoulders.
- *Line managers*: Talking to your line manager (head of department, mentor, deptuty head, etc.) is very important. He/she
  will be able to take practical measures to reassure you, reduce
  your workload or alleviate pressure. If you do not feel comfortable talking to your line manager, then discuss the matter
  with a senior colleague whom you do get on with.
- *Family and friends*: As the people closest to you, they will want
  to help, whether offering support or simply reminding you of
  the good things in life. Let them know how you are feeling.
  People often take out their frustrations on their nearest and
  dearest – before you lash out, stop and think about what it is
  you are really angry about.
- *Unions*: The teaching unions are on your side. They campaign
  about issues such as this, and will be a useful source of advice
  and guidance. Your school will have a union rep, but if you
  would rather talk to an outsider you can contact your regional
  office.
- *Occupational health*: Your school may refer you to the local
  occupational health team. Again, these individuals are on your
  side. They may get involved in monitoring your situation,
  ensuring that the authority is doing what they can to support
  you. Some may also provide a counselling service.
- *GP*: It is important that you make your GP aware of work-
  related stress problems. Stress can have a profound effect on an
  individual's health. Complications such as high blood pressure, digestive disorders, ulcers, heart attack and depression are
  all associated with stress. Your GP can give you a thorough

check-up. They will also be responsible for signing you off work, should this become the case.

Worst–case scenario

If stress has taken its toll you may be advised by your GP to take time off. If you are in bad way this could be an extensive period of time. Usually such advice is greeted with mixed emotions: primarily relief – but this is often accompanied by anxiety. How will this affect your career prospects? What will colleagues think? How could you let your students down? What will you *do* for the next six weeks? Time off for stress is not like time off for holidays. Stress-related suffering has a tendency to hijack your entire body and mind – it is not pleasant and it leaves little room for fun. Recovery should be your priority: resting, relaxing, reflecting and, quite likely, re-evaluating what you want from your life and your job.

As you return to work, make sure you are ready. Ease yourself into it gradually and do not expect things to instantly feel normal. It is likely your nerves will still be pretty jangled. You will be comforted, if not a little overwhelmed, by how supportive the staff are – and you may be pleasantly surprised by the reaction of your students. However, do expect to fend off the bizarre rumours that will have circulated in your absence: Sir has had time off to appear on *Big Brother*/Miss has had a baby (in a month?).

With time, you will establish your rhythm again, but be careful not to slip back into old, unhealthy ways. Make the changes you need to, in both your work and personal life, in order to manage and cope and enjoy what you do. You may decide to release yourself from additional roles and responsibilities. You may decide to devote less time to work, and to focus on family life. You may decide to get a job in another school. Or you may decide that teaching is not for you. Whatever you decide, it is the right decision. If there is one good thing to come out of stress-related illness it is that it can make a person realize what really matters to them.

Having a life outside of school

I should not really have to write a section about how to enjoy yourself when you are not working, but I hear so many young teachers complaining that they do not have time for anything other than school in their lives, it makes me worry. Your job is important, but it is not the sum total of your existence. Besides, do you really get paid enough to spend every evening and every weekend 'catching up' on paperwork? Didn't think so.

In order to do a good job it is often necessary to put in some additional hours, but when the extent of these hours stops you from having time for your family, your friends and for yourself, something is amiss. Keep your work–life balance in check. Work out what is essential, try to complete as much of it as you can during the school day, and learn to say no to non-essential tasks. If you are the kind of person who is driven by steady perfectionism it may be time to let go of your whim – no amount of ruthlessly careful planning can guarantee a perfect lesson. It will certainly help to structure your teaching but, ultimately, what happens in the classroom is more important than what happens on paper. A far more useful habit to develop would be spontaneity: the ability to perform in the unpredictable immediacy of the moment.

As for school holidays – make the most of them. Although we quietly try to shirk off the envy of non-teaching friends – we work through the holidays/we *need* the holidays/we are too tired to appreciate them – let's face it, school holidays are a real bonus. Knowing that you will never complete more than an eight-week stretch without a week's break is a comforting thought (and it makes the ritual practice of counting down days till the end of term easier). Holidays are an important opportunity to allow your body and mind to recover from the rigours of the previous term, and gather energy for the next, helping you to combat cumulative stress. Whatever you enjoy doing, do plenty of it – you've earned it.

When life outside is the problem

Sometimes home life can be the cause of significant stress. Family demands, relationship breakdowns, bereavement, moving house or other personal worries can make life very difficult at times. For some, this may make school feel like sanctuary. For others, having to walk into a classroom and behave as though nothing is wrong can be very draining. You simply want to cry – instead you have to get excited about prime numbers.

Teaching is much like acting. It is a performance, one that relies on you to interact with your audience and get them doing things. It requires energy and concentration. If you are not feeling good in yourself, finding that energy can be very tough. If some of your darlings are particularly challenging the strain will be even greater. From my experience, one of the hardest aspects of working with BESD students is having to provide a consistently calming, neutral influence – no matter how you are feeling personally.

If you are having a bad time, consider letting a trusted colleague know – they will be able to look out for you, and defend any erratic behaviour. Relieve the pressure on yourself by preparing a few 'easy' lessons – wheel out the video player, or get them doing something low key: silent reading, independent creative writing, computer work or research projects. But do not become one of those teachers who uses the captive audience of the classroom to unload their personal problems. Your students do not need to know how selfish your current girlfriend is – they really don't have the answers you are looking for!

Part Six

In the Staffroom

Staffrooms are the nucleus of school life, a place where you can hide from the students and find adult company, a space to concentrate quietly or take the weight off your feet and relax for a while. In larger schools it is increasingly common for staffrooms to be departmentalized; in other words, each department or subject area has its own self-sufficient space. On the plus side, this can create closer unity within departments; on the negative, it removes the 'buzz' of a whole-staff meeting place and has the potential to be quite divisive.

Staffrooms are sustained by the contributions of the people in them, and often reflect the atmosphere of the environment at large. Tensions between management, too much out-of-control student behaviour, cramped classrooms – all will manifest themselves in the mood of the staffroom. On the other hand, supportive management, good exam results, firm behaviour policies: the staffroom feels optimistic. Hopefully this is characteristic of your school, but if not, all is not lost. Staffroom atmospheres are not necessarily stable – people come and go, feelings change. What was once a grumpy place can become a happy one, and vice versa.

This part of the book looks at the roles other staff members will play in your school career – how to be a team player, and how to get the best, and deal with the worst, of staffroom antics.

17 Professionalism

Sharing information

Keeping each other informed helps a team to work smoothly. Sometimes, however, it is easier said than done. Everyone is busy. Everyone has somewhere to be, or something to do. Just tracking people down can prove difficult enough. It is important, therefore, that staff find ways of getting messages through to one another even when they cannot speak directly.

The faithful student messenger still has its place (I can remember the honour: taking a note to the school secretary was like being asked to carry the crown jewels), as do Post-its in pigeon-holes. But these days, technology is catching up with us. We have internal phone systems, email and, for the senior management big guys, walkie-talkies – all designed to make the sharing of information easier and quicker. There is still, however, a lot to be said for having a good old-fashioned face-to-face conversation. But about what? The sort of information you need to think about sharing includes:

- *Concerns about student welfare:* If you know that a student is having some personal difficulties, for instance arguments with friends, or illness in the family, it may be helpful to discreetly inform other staff, so that they may take this into account. 'Discreet' is the operative word – if issues are of a sensitive nature you should first inform your CPO and seek further advice from them.
- *Incidents of problematic behaviour:* If you have just endured a particularly difficult lesson, or had to deal with a significant incident of poor behaviour, it can be helpful to forewarn the next poor soul that has to teach them. Send a brief note with a trustworthy student or catch up with them during a break.

- *Rumours or emerging disputes:* Occasionally you may be tipped off about some sort of lunchtime happening being planned among the students. I have known of whole year groups staging mass walkouts, or attacking each other in gangs. Mob rule is difficult to contain, but if you pick up on any such scheming ensure that you alert other members of staff – strength in numbers.
- *Student sensitivities and needs:* The fact that you have got to know a difficult student and developed some successful strategies for managing them does not mean that other teachers will have the opportunity, or the inclination, to do the same; yet they may, from time to time, have to deal with that student. If you can make a point of sharing some of the strategies that get a positive response you will be helping both the staff and the student.
- *Staff/timetable/room changes:* If you need to make an arrangement or a swap with another staff member, organize it as far in advance as possible. Making last-minute changes can be frustrating and stressful.
- *Good news:* Why not let a tutor/head of year know that their class has improved or done well? Make a point of mentioning individual or group achievements during staff meetings. Within the struggles, it is always nice to hear something positive.

Sharing responsibilities

Teaching can seem like a fairly lonesome profession. It gives you the independence to do as and what you will in your own classroom, but it is sometimes nice to know that there are other teachers out there. Although you may work by yourself (people below the age of consent do not count!) in your own room for many hours of the working day, you are still part of a team. They can help you, and you can help them. OK. So some of them have dirty beards. One of them smells funny, and the other one looks like Alistair Crowley, but at the end of the day they are your department – learn to love them!

Goodwill, good communication and good support are vital to the functioning of an effective group of staff. This applies at both a whole-school and departmental level. Cooperation makes life easier for everyone; it also leads to more consistent practice across the school, which is beneficial to the overall ethos of the environment. You and the staff you work with can help each other in a number of ways, be it on an emotional, practical or theoretical level:

- *Planning and preparation:* Individual departments operate in different ways. Some may expect everyone to teach the same schemes of work at the same time. Others will allow more freedom to choose. If schemes of work can be planned as a group the burden is shared. Each person could take on several schemes, for which to plan and gather resources, then pass copies on to the other members of staff. Why have six people reproducing the same information? If you are a small department you could try linking up with nearby schools.

- *Assessment:* If assessment can be looked at as a group the chances of it being delivered consistently are increased. At the beginning of a teaching career it is often difficult to interpret what constitutes poor, adequate and good standards of work for any given age group. The opportunity to work alongside more experienced staff will give you insight into how to distinguish your triumphs from your tragedies.

- *Troubleshooting:* Having trouble with Luke in class 5? Don't know what to do with the girl gang in class 10? A few brains can be better than one when trying to solve tricky problems. 'Workshop' sessions, in which staff examine a particular scenario and then explore possible solutions, can be really useful. There is, sadly, far too little opportunity for teachers to get together and spend time making coherent, collective plans to deal with the common issues that plague them.

- *Sharing skills and knowledge:* Most schools will have a mix of teachers – some new, some with years of experience – providing a range of insights and wisdoms. Staff from abroad, staff with specific subject specialisms, staff from different cultural backgrounds: a wealth of information is available to you.

Supporting each other

Who knows what teachers have to put up with better than other teachers? Support and camaraderie among staff can make a huge difference to the working day. On an informal level, the staffroom banter can ease away stress and help keep things in perspective. Knowing that there is a group of friendly faces in your corner of the staffroom, who are ready to empathize with your sickening dread of class 7B, and who utterly agree that the new deputy head is smarmy, is a great comfort when times are tough.

Support between colleagues also plays a role in the overall management of the school. Anyone who has worked in an BESD unit will know that the way in which staff support one another is crucial. Without teamwork and solidarity, the task of managing challenging behaviour becomes very difficult. If you are faced with a difficult situation, perhaps a fight or conflict, it is a relief to have someone step into the arena with you – or at least to know they are available should you require them. Making an offer of assistance to a staff member in need shows goodwill – one day the karma will come back to you! Have you ever noticed how the least helpful teachers tend to be the grumpiest ones?

18 And beyond

Making friends

The lighter side of staffroom etiquette is, of course, that it gives you the opportunity to nurture some sort of social life out of the wreckage of the school day. Whether you are looking to establish a whole new set of best mates, or simply wanting to have a few laughs with like-minded people during your breaks, most school environments will provide what you are looking for. However, friend-making potential does seem to vary from school to school. If you are about to join somewhere new, do not automatically assume that the staffroom atmosphere will be as bouncy, or listless, as your previous establishment. Some places are instantly friendly, but in others it may take time to infiltrate the social scene.

Within my experiences of different schools I have come across a few recurring characteristics. Some schools have a 'young' staff: lots of NQTs and trainees, many of whom will be youthful enough to still know what the inside of a nightclub looks like. The plus side is lots of fun and enthusiasm. The down, is that general inexperience and regular hangovers mean hard work for everyone. Some schools will seem mildly institutionalized: teachers who have taught in the same classroom, sat in the same staffroom chair, and worn the same suit for the past ten years! This can be a good sign: stability is healthy and people are contented enough to stay put, but to an outsider it may feel somewhat stagnant. The fact that many schools employ overseas staff has perhaps been rather good for teachers of a social persuasion. If you are living temporarily in a new country, you may well look to make the most of the opportunity, and play as hard as you work. Schools with a high intake of overseas staff often have lively social scenes – good for the atmosphere, bad for the liver!

The ultimate question is, do you want to be friends with a bunch of teachers? Or do you prefer not to blur the boundaries of work and personal life? Is the annual staff 'do' just about as much as you can take? If so, then avoid all eye contact and keep your mouth to yourself.

Making more than just friends

When I was young, I believed there was some kind of conspiracy going on. My parents were both teachers, all their friends were teachers, and all their friends' friends were teachers. And what happened to me? I became a teacher, met a non-teacher, and managed to break the cycle (or so I thought). Within a year of knowing him, my delightfully unconventional non-teacher decided to follow the pathway to the classroom door. As far as I am concerned, the conspiracy still stands!

A career in teaching can be more than just a job – it has the ability to shape your lifestyle and identity, should you let it. It is no wonder, really, that teachers often end up in relationships with other teachers, with whom they can share the holidays, bitch about government policies, and instinctively understand what it is to have a 'bad day at the office'. Romance in the staffroom can be a beautiful thing, oh yes, but it also has its fair share of obstacles:

- *Dealing with gossip:* Whether your blossoming relationship is surrounded by scandal and controversy or not, do not be surprised if you become the subject of staffroom gossip (until something more interesting comes along!). The merest hint of workplace romance will inevitably cause some excitement – usually good-natured curiosity – but occasionally something more malicious will circulate. Ride the gossip wave with dignity. The talk will fade faster if you do not do anything to fuel it.
- *Going public:* One way to put a rumour to bed is to set the record straight. If your relationship has become suitably serious, it may be helpful to let a few key members of staff know (line managers, your department). An informal chat is all that is needed – no need to make a whole-staff announcement in the morning briefing (yet). Even if you feel your

courtship bears no relevance to your work in school, unless you are extremely careful it will be noticed. Far better that your closest colleagues hear it from you, rather than from the casual gossip.

- *Dealing with curious students:* 'So-and-so from class 10 said they saw you and Mr Jakes holding hands in the cinema queue on Sunday . . . then they saw you kissing. My mum says you're not even divorced yet!' The best advice, if you wish to canoodle with your staffroom love in public, is to live several towns away from your students. Failing that, buy yourselves some convincing disguises.

- *Strictly professional:* Be careful not to become so loved-up that you forget where you are. Love may be blind, but the caretaker isn't, and it is unlikely that he or she would care to see two middle-aged teachers sloppy kissing in the ICT room after hours. Without careful treatment, staffroom romance can easily become rather unsavoury. What seems like a romantic thrill to you may be deeply disturbing to others – save it for your private world.

- *Breaking up is never easy:* Oh, the sadness! Education's answer to *Romeo and Juliet* has fallen by the wayside. All that is left, now that the heart-shaped Post-its have been torn up, is the small matter of you both having to share a staffroom together. Can you be friends? Or are you sick of the sight of each other? Once again, it is necessary to put professional dignity before personal politics – no public rows, backstabbing or snide remarks. You brought this situation into the workplace, therefore it is up to you to manage it responsibly. If you can both agree to deal with any emotional overspill by meeting to discuss things in a venue away from work there is less chance of it interfering with school life.

As if you have the chance . . .

Here I am, informing you of all the hundreds of things you need to be doing in order to be a good teacher, and now I am trying to convince you that you also have time for friends and a love life!

19 Dealing with difficulties

Conflict

Although teachers are generally known to be very supportive towards one another, tensions will sometimes arise. Staffrooms can bring together an unlikely mix of people, who will have come into teaching for a variety of reasons and from a diverse range of backgrounds. Different expectations, different styles and different experiences will inevitably create strain within the team spirit from time to time. If you feel you are caught up or even steeped in work colleague conflict, consider this advice:

- *Practise being 'open':* A culture in which you feel comfortable about raising concerns or objections is healthier than one in which you feel you should keep your thoughts to yourself, in order to avoid causing trouble. The key is in knowing *how* to express yourself. Think of the terms that apply to communicating with students: calm, firm, fair and constructive – it should be no different when talking to adults. If you have an opinion to express, being poised and diplomatic in this way will increase the chances of others respecting your views. If you rant and complain, or try to steamroller people with your argument, they will only notice your temperament.
- *Try to empathize:* Sometimes decisions will be made or opinions expressed that you do not particularly like. But before you dismiss them it is worth trying to put yourself in the shoes of the person who made them. What is their role? What are they trying to achieve? For example, senior staff members sometimes have to make controversial decisions in order to serve the greater good. Empathy, of course, should be a universal tool – if you are willing to understand why a decision

has to be made, the decision maker should be willing to understand why it bothers you.

- *Deal with tense meetings:* There is nothing like a departmental meeting, after a long day of teaching, to bring underlying arguments to the surface. And there is nothing more frustrating than having to sit through a staff meeting that is dominated by arguments and personal vendettas. Meetings should not be war zones, they are an opportunity to try to move forward and find solutions. If conflict emerges, hopefully the chair will be able to refocus everyone on the meeting agenda and maintain momentum. If necessary, an additional meeting should be called, or time set aside at the end, in order to tackle the issues surrounding the conflict.

- *Be self-aware:* If a staff member approaches you in an argumentative manner, or makes a statement that bothers you, know the measure of your reaction before you give it. Are you likely to lose your temper, feel mortally offended, or give a bitchy retort? Is your reaction intended to incite further conflict rather than defuse it? If you do not feel capable of giving the sort of response that shows what a stable, responsible and well-adjusted individual you are, try deferring your reaction: 'I think we need to discuss this further, but I am not able to do that at the moment – let's arrange to talk later.'

Bullying

Studies suggest that a significant proportion of recorded workplace bullying incidents occur within the teaching profession. It seems odd to think that education, which actively participates in developing the attitudes and minds of young people and promotes anti-bullying policies, should be a breeding ground for bullying among adults. Is it not simply a case of practising what we preach?

Unfortunately, the answer is no. Bullying behaviour has a complicated network of motivations. Cast an eye around your staffroom and notice the enormous variety of personality types: the bossy ones, the earnest ones, the stirrers and the gossips, the argumentative ones, the lazy ones, the gobby ones, the quiet ones – all working as part of a 'team', often under considerable pressure. Within this cacophony of odd-bodies not everyone will have developed the capacity to value and respect the feelings of others, or to be aware of themselves and the way they relate to the world. They may be power seekers, frustrated control freaks, who are compelled to emphasize their 'greatness' over others in order to cover up weakness. They may be sheep, desperate to belong and, therefore, happy to go along with whatever the gang does, even if that means picking on others. They may be jealous. They may be emotionally damaged. They may be so self-absorbed they do not see how their actions can be anything other than right.

Bullies project their own inadequacies, anxieties and fears on to others, by engaging in behaviour that seeks to belittle, isolate or cause distress to their target. This is neither fair nor acceptable. When it occurs in the workplace it destroys morale, damages confidence and causes stress. As well as affecting individual victims, it can be detrimental to the atmosphere of the whole school, creating bad feeling and tension. If you, or a colleague, are suffering at the hands of a workplace bully, it is important to take action.

- Keep a private record of conversations/incidents between you and the bully – note the time, date and location, and the names of anyone that could have witnessed them.
- Talk to a senior member of staff whom you trust, and find out what they propose to do about it.
- Talk to your union, who will be able to give advice, inform you of your rights and help you to confront the situation.

If your school/authority has effective procedures for dealing with workplace bullying you may feel well supported and able to continue as normal – once the situation has been resolved. Unfortunately not all schools are clued up, and in some, workplace bullying is fairly institutionalized. You may also be in a situation where the bully is, in fact, one of your managers. This is why it is so important to seek advice from your union – they represent you and your needs.

Staff at any level can be bullies, or bullied. Victims are not necessarily the weedy and vulnerable; often those that are successful, popular and well adjusted are targeted. Bullying can also take many forms. It may be blatant, or it may be insidious and secretive – sometimes it can seem as though no one notices it but you.

A bully may use a number of ways to get at you. Here are some examples:

- criticizing you in front of your students, or your peers;
- blaming you unfairly for any problems;
- interfering with your work practice, for example changing your timetable, giving you unpleasant or menial tasks;
- checking up on you excessively or implying mistrust in your competence;
- making unreasonable demands on your workload, or making it difficult for you to carry out certain tasks;
- making negative or dismissive remarks about your contributions, and making comments that undermine you;
- making comments that attack or ridicule your appearance, personality or work;
- attempting to isolate you socially, and make other staff dislike you;
- playing practical jokes against your wishes, or deliberately trying to cause you embarrassment;
- spreading malicious rumours about you;
- Sexually harassing you.

Sometimes a bully's behaviour can seem to verge on the ridiculous – their vendetta becomes so intense that they have to react to every little thing you do or say. You walk into the room, and they start to huff and puff in absolute disgust. At this you can only laugh, and pity them for their sad, pathetic, unhappy existence. If you are a victim of bullying, never listen to the voice that tries to tell you it is your own fault, and remind yourself that the reason the bully is targeting you is that you have something that they need: good values.

Carrying weak staff

As you move away from the shakier ground that is trodden by the NQT, and begin to establish yourself as a pivotal member of your teaching team, you may discover that you are one of the strongest. The pleasant realization that you are, in fact, very competent at what you do will boost your confidence and perhaps trigger thoughts of promotion. It will also, however, awaken you to the frustration of

having to work alongside people who are less efficient, less conscientious and less effective than you. If you are in any way reliant
on other members of your team, for their commitment, their contributions or their organization, it can feel as though you are at their
mercy: the staff member who, week after week, fails to turn up at
your jointly run after-school club; the teaching assistant who cannot
put a poster up straight, let alone be responsible for whole-class
organization; or the head of year who always disappears at the first
sniff of trouble, leaving you to fend for yourself.

Here are some suggestions on how to manage the burden of
'carrying' weaker members of staff. Of course, if the person fails to
make improvements or is a chronic drain on the rest of the team the
issue may need to be raised with senior managers.

- *Encouragement:* Instead of complaining about what they do not
  get right, think about ways in which you can motivate them.
  Using positive reinforcement (as you would with your students) is just as applicable to work colleagues. 'I really appreciate your help first thing in the morning – it makes the rest
  of the day so much easier' is more enticing than 'I'm fed up
  with you getting in late'.
- *Show them how you want things done:* Sometimes it is worth
  investing a bit of time demonstrating or modelling your
  expectations, for instance how an activity needs to be completed or how to communicate with a difficult student – don't
  assume that your colleagues will automatically know because
  you do. If you can give them some guidance you will give
  them confidence and increase the chances of them getting it
  right.
- *Be inclusive:* Talk about situations with reference to what 'we'
  do, as opposed to singling out the individual: 'When *we* leave
  the staffroom in a mess . . .' or 'When *we* help each other . . .'.
  This emphasizes team effort and unity, avoiding the implication that one person is better than another – which only leads
  to resentment and division.
- *Avoid them:* An alternative approach to coping with a less than
  competent colleague is to keep your involvement with them
  to a minimum, if it is possible. This way their poor standards
  of input are less likely to affect your work.

- *Exercise your judgement:* While it is important to show solidarity and support for colleagues when dealing with rude or unacceptable student behaviour, sometimes it is necessary to be judicious in the way you respond. Some of your colleagues may be unduly aggressive or unpleasant in the way they communicate with students, resulting in unnecessary confrontation. Remain neutral.

Gossip, backstabbing and cliques

Unfortunately we do not live in a perfect world. Even the bubbliest of staffrooms can have an undercurrent of menace: cliques, schisms and power games. The elite, power-dressing modern foreign languages department, who are 'in' with the head and sneer at everyone else. The two tribes of Key Stage 2: Mrs Dovecote versus Miss Petal – opposite corners of the staffroom, marker pens at dawn. Or factions within the senior management team: petty squabbles over dinner duty getting in the way of real work. Some people allow their personal agendas to dominate their experience of the workplace – they preoccupy themselves with bitching or one-upmanship, as though it somehow adds colour to their lives. At least the autonomous nature of teaching means that you can easily retreat to your classroom and escape the clutches of staffroom politics.

So unless you are one of those people who likes to stir things up and watch tension unfold, you may be best advised to keep neutral and stay away from the trouble spots. Staffroom conflicts, whether up-front or covert, can create an unpleasant atmosphere and, if allowed to fester, will interfere with staff effectiveness. Of course, it can be hard to resist the temptation to blow off steam and join in with a bitching tirade against the detached and bone-idle head of department, who creates more problems than he solves – but ultimately what will this achieve? If you truly want a situation to change, think about how you can take proactive steps to achieve this, and carefully make your concerns explicit to the person in question.

Part Seven

How to Win Friends and Influence . . .

It is not just staff and students that you will have to deal with during your teaching career – parents/carers are part of the equation too. This part of the book looks at how to work with different 'types' of parental concern: the ones who get involved, the ones who get too involved, and the ones who do not seem to bother at all. It goes on to consider how to build working relationships with that other important group of people who have a vested interest in your work: senior management. As the title suggests, some of this information is concerned with how to impress – getting yourself noticed for the right reasons may be the doorway to opportunity and promotion.

20 The parents

Making contact

Teachers have varying amounts of contact with the parents/carers of their students. Primary or special school staff may have daily contact, as children are collected from school by family members. Others may have less frequent involvement – the occasional telephone call or letter, and a five-minute slot during parents' evenings. In an ideal world we would be able to develop very strong, healthy links between school and home life. Both of these environments are pivotal in a young person's development, therefore it is important that they both strive to provide a continuum of support: shared expectations of conduct, attitude and values; joint promotion of the importance of education; and mutual understanding of the way in which these things are best achieved.

The reality, however, is somewhat compromised. Many people, both school staff and families, work tirelessly to achieve a continuum of support, but are up against challenges. Schools may be unsympathetic to the struggles faced by parents; some parents are unduly antagonistic towards staff members. Some schools may fail to support the needs of individual students; while some parents undermine the work of teachers by failing to reinforce appropriate boundaries for their children.

For the teacher, the realization that any boundaries, values and expectations can be instantly unravelled the moment the student steps out of the school gates is frustrating. It is not just a matter of getting the students on side, but the parents as well – and this can prove difficult. We have to understand that some parents/carers will have a tainted opinion of school, due to their own negative experiences. They may be wary or suspicious of such establishments, and will fail to see how schooling can have a positive impact on their offspring.

Some adults may feel insecure or ashamed of their own lack of academic ability, and will therefore feel intimidated by the education world. Fortunately schools are continuing to develop ways in which to overcome such barriers, and open themselves up to the wider community: parent groups, parent assistance in the classroom and on trips, after-school clubs and activities that involve other adults in the community, adult learning groups, evening classes and open days.

As a teacher you can help ease the lines of communication by ensuring that, when you speak to the significant others in your students' lives, you are polite and diplomatic. Give an honest account of what is happening/what progress the child is making – try to use concrete evidence to support your views (such as examples of work, a list of homework marks, a log of incidents). Avoid using teaching jargon, as this can be off-putting, and try to suggest some future targets for the student. If you have to report bad news (for example that a child has not completed homework or has been involved in an incident), remind yourself that it can be distressing for parents to discover that their little angels have been up to no good – speak calmly and express regret. Your aim is to get the parent on your side.

Those who want to know . . .

Your first ever parents' evening can be a daunting experience. Hopefully, your mentor will give you the opportunity to sit with them and watch how a pro does it, before leaving you on your own. Once you get used to the process it is not scary at all, in fact it is sometimes quite interesting – meeting a child's parents will often explain quite a lot! Parents/carers fall loosely into two categories: those who take an interest in their child's schooling and those who, for whatever reasons, keep well clear. Some are a joy to work with – others just create obstacles. There is a well-known assumption that resurfaces every time a parents' evening is due: the parents you desperately need to see (their child has fallen behind/caused lots of problems/destroyed everything) will not turn up. Here are some descriptions of the type of parents you might encounter, starting with those who, for better or for worse, like to get involved:

- *The perfect ones:* Supportive, cooperative, available and understanding – this is the parent of your dreams. Always willing to help out and appreciative of your input, they make you feel like a good teacher and often let you know how much their son/daughter loves your lessons.

- *The ultra-defensive ones:* Over-protective and somewhat conceited, they believe their child is utterly perfect. The ones who refuse to accept that 'little Tyler' had anything to do with the vandalism in the girls' toilets: 'Well, I can assure you, she's not like that at home . . .' (the implication being that it is your fault).

- *The pushy ones:* Interfering and demanding, these are the parents who are convinced their child is a genius, and should therefore receive more attention, more work and more input then any other child in the class. They take every opportunity to tell you how you should be doing your job, but fail to notice how their excessively high expectations are turning their son/daughter into a nervous wreck.

- *The helpless ones:* Needy and vulnerable, these parents are sometimes bullied by their own children, victims of their circumstances. They consequently look to you for support and help, and will call on you at all times of the day asking for advice – never give them your personal phone number! Their intentions are generally good, but their over-dependence can be frustrating.

- *The teacher ones:* Eek! Sitting face to face with the parent-teacher of one of your students can leave you wondering whether they are empathizing with you, admiring your dedication or exposing you for a fraud. And there is nothing more toe curling than having to explain to a fellow professional that their son/daughter is a complete hell-raiser!

And those who don't

- *The unavailable ones:* Parents who fail to turn up for meetings, avoid all communication, and always have an excuse as to why they cannot collect their child or attend a school event – which makes life difficult when a problem arises or support is needed.

- *The busy ones:* Those who regularly turn up to meetings or collect their children twenty minutes late, looking harassed

and explaining how crazy the traffic was – which is little consolation to you, having missed your own train in order to fulfil
your duty-of-care obligation, and to their child, who snivels
in the corner, thinking mummy is never coming.

- *The 'you deal with it' ones:* They sit opposite you, looking non-
chalant and bored, and then declare that it is not their
problem, what are they supposed to do about it, whatever,
boys will be boys . . . enough said!

- *The unhelpful ones:* Parents who do not recognize that learning begins in the home – that the nurture and encouragement
a child receives within their family environment will influence
that child's feelings about education. Reading with him for
ten minutes a day, to help him catch up with the others.
Making sure she gets her homework done on time. Is it really
too much to ask, considering the difference it could make?

- *The difficult ones:* Adults who hate the concept of school and
all its employees, and will be confrontational, or even aggressive, whenever they are invited (or in some cases uninvited) to
share their views with teaching staff. If you are faced with an
angry or irrational parent, explain that you will only be able
to talk with them when they are calm – suggest arranging a
meeting for another time, and ask for another staff member to
be present.

21 Senior management

An enviable task?

Uniting a large group of staff is an undeniably difficult task. I have yet to discover a school in which every single employee has nothing to complain about when it comes to management. I have worked with some wonderful managers, but even they have not been able to please all of the people all of the time. A good management team will strive to balance the interests and needs of staff, students and parents, in ways that unite and inspire. They will provide strong leadership. They will listen. They will consult. And they will be visible, approachable figureheads. Nevertheless, they may sometimes have to make choices that upset certain individuals.

The real problems begin when members of the management team are actually useless at what they do. Bad management can have a devastating effect on the atmosphere and morale of a school; and unfortunately, once an individual has reached leadership status they tend to be set in their ways – unlikely to turn around and say 'You're right . . . I have been behaving like an evil tyrant this past year. I'll take anger management classes and change!' Reasons to complain about your rogue senior managers:

- good at financial management, *bad* at people management;
- good at people management, *bad* at financial management;
- weak leadership;
- patronizing staff during meetings, and telling them off like students;
- never 'available', and disappearing just when you need them;
- not knowing the names of staff, but extolling the importance of you knowing the names of your students;

- wasting money on glossy promotion of themselves and the school, when some departments do not even have textbooks;
- favouring some subjects/staff over others, and making no secret of this;
- making drastic changes without consulting others;
- failing to support or back up staff, in favour of parents or students;
- telling lies;
- taking power dressing to unnecessary extremes.

Getting noticed

Now that you are surviving in the classroom, you may want to start thinking about your future. Do you want to climb the ranks, increase your salary, give yourself new challenges or broaden your experience? Are you hungry for status or do you simply want to stretch your talents? Wherever you see yourself in ten years' time, your starting point is the here and now. This section is a light-hearted look at how to demonstrate that you are worthy of promotion and impress those who matter:

- *Get involved:* Management like staff who show commitment to the school and its aims. The most effective way to display undying love for your establishment is to make continuous contributions to school life: join the PTA, run an after-school club, be a school fundraising enthusiast, make dynamic comments during training days, and be sure to attend every single parents' evening/presentation day on the calendar.
- *Be reliable:* Be on time for meetings, preferably early so that you can show further willing by putting out chairs or organizing coffee. Get your reports in a week before the due date. Have the only form group who hand in all of their reply slips. Empty your pigeon-hole daily (which will imply that you are well organized). Leave an immaculate set of lesson plans on your desk each night, just in case you fall ill the following day – though never actually be ill.
- *Take initiative:* Show them that you are more than just a follower. Demonstrate your leadership potential by taking control at chaotic departmental meetings. Make snappy suggestions

and use phrases such as 'solution focused', 'empowerment' and 'overcoming barriers'. Organize events such as football tournaments and read-a-thons. Do not sit around gossiping in the staffroom, and try to give others the impression that there is always something exciting going on in your lessons.

- *Never complain:* Management are interested in people who will cooperate with them, so show unbridled support for any suggestion the head teacher makes. Offer to do the jobs that no one else wants to do, such as gate duty at the school disco, or detaining the naughty students during activity week. And make sure no one ever catches you bad-mouthing school policies.

Just be careful that, in your bid to make yourself indispensable, you do not become one of those ageing, 'never-was' teachers – a lifetime of crawling that has got you nowhere. Believe it or not there are some ruthless managers out there, who will simply take advantage of someone who shows willing: 'Oh, Mr Brown. He's always happy to organize the school fete . . .'. Ensure that your efforts lead to a promotion rather than a plateau, by letting your managers know that your have aspirations. The best way to do this? More crawling: 'I'm really inspired by the way you've developed your career. It would be great if you could give me some expert advice.'

Beyond Survival

Part Eight

Getting the Most from your Classroom

By now you will be a competent and confident teacher. With three or more years of classroom practice under your belt the things that used to worry you as an NQT will seem a distant memory. Lesson planning, behaviour management, organizing your workload, talking to parents, motivating your students – it is all within your grasp. You now have the satisfaction of watching other fledgling teachers make the same mistakes and have the same struggles, knowing that it is all behind you – you have earned your stripes. They come to you for advice. They respect you. Even the students have new-found reverence for you. They have seen you around, their brothers and sisters have been taught by you. You are now a fixture. But before you start thinking that from now on it will be easy . . . you now have the chance to turn from a competent teacher into a *great* teacher! This part of the book provides hints and ideas on how to give a further boost to your classroom practice, and how to maximize the potential of all of your students.

22 Refining your skills

Evaluating your strengths and weaknesses

Perhaps the best place to start, when considering how to develop your skills in the classroom, is to establish an understanding of your strengths and weaknesses. Some people are instinctively aware of what these are; others will need to spend some time reflecting on their practice in order to figure this out. If you are one of these people, there are a number of ways in which you can do this:

- *Mentoring/appraisal*: If your authority/school has a good programme of continuing professional development (CPD), they will provide you with support and guidance beyond your induction year, helping you to clarify your goals and analyse the way in which you have coped with various situations. You may be given an annual appraisal, often involving a lesson observation and interview. This should not be a case of passively listening to someone telling you what they think of your work – it should be a dialogue, an opportunity for you to ask questions, get advice, identify areas for development and agree on how this will take place.
- *Self-reflection*: Much can be learned from making personal observations of the way in which you manage situations (see the advice on reflective practice in Part Two). Pay attention to the times that feel stressful: what is happening? Are you having trouble with some of your more difficult students? Are your students continually complaining that your lessons are boring? Do you get flustered over lesson content? And what about the times that feel good? Your class are grasping a complicated idea, or one of your most difficult students makes a genuine effort – what is the secret of your success?

- *Peer observations*: Sometimes objective onlookers will be able to identify strengths and weaknesses that you are not able to see for yourself. Allowing a trusted colleague to observe your teaching, and then give you some practitioner-to-practitioner feedback can be very refreshing. See the next section for further information about peer observation.
- *Ask your students*: Who better to comment on your performance than the very people it affects? If you are not ready to face a direct onslaught of comments about whether they like you or not, the information can be extracted surreptitiously. At the end of a project or task, give students an evaluation sheet to fill out, asking broad questions such as 'How motivated do you feel in these lessons? Do you feel that you are able to work peacefully? What would you do to improve the atmosphere of this classroom?' Of course, you will get some silly answers ('not very, don't care, ban work'), but you may also receive a few helpful insights, and words of encouragement.

Once you have identified areas for development you will need to find ways of challenging yourself to tackle them. It may be helpful to outline some targets. Keep them simple and achievable: 'To develop the use of time-out with students in class 6' or 'To set up more efficient class routines for organizing and putting away equipment during practical sessions'. Perhaps your objectives will be more long term: 'To improve understanding of the needs of SEN students in the year group' or 'To undertake a course in positive behaviour management and develop expertise in this area'.

Peer observations

Peer observations are an effective way of sharing skills and spreading examples of good practice across the teaching profession. Undoubtedly, some teachers will be resistant to the idea of having other adults in their classroom, such is the legacy of Ofsted inspection – another teacher scrutinizing your practice, invading the private world of your classroom, and exposing all your flaws? How hideous! But beyond the fragile and insecure, many teachers see the benefits of peer observation – a chance to get an objective opinion from someone who actually knows what they are talking about; and if you are the observer, a chance to see how others do it, which will either give you confidence (you are better than them!) or new ideas (they are better than you!).

Peer observations can be cross-curricular, between different year groups, or between teachers with very different styles. The most helpful ones are perhaps those that are carried out between teachers who have particular interest in each other's work: maybe from the same department, or dealing with the same kind of problems. They may be organized formally, or perhaps you can set them up yourself. A group of you might want to establish a peer observation cycle, taking turns to observe each other and allowing you to gain insight into a variety of different approaches and practices.

It is helpful to work with people who you trust and respect – who will give you an honest but supportive account of your classroom practice. Peer observation is not necessarily about watching an expert or someone with more experience. It is about mutual support and encouragement between staff members, enabling you to learn from each other and solve problems together.

An alternative to peer observation is the shadowing of another staff member. If you have decided you would like to develop your understanding of a certain role within school, for example SENCO or head of year, it may be beneficial to arrange a day, or a few hours a week shadowing them – and discovering what the job involves from an insider's perspective. This will help to prepare you for future promotion, and give you further insight into whether a role is for you or not.

Experimenting with approaches

You spend weeks putting together what you believe is a fantastic activity. You run yourself ragged looking for useful resources. It will all be worth it in the end, you tell yourself. The lesson comes round and, well, they spend most of their time ogling a group of sixth-formers sunbathing on the grass outside.

But now that you have stacks of confidence there is plenty you can do to keep your students interested and your learning activities fresh. You may have found a comfort zone within your teaching: a lesson formula that is easy to deliver and gets results. This is a good thing (providing stability and consistency), until the soul drops out of it: it becomes predictable and dull, for you and your students. If you feel you have been playing it safe for too long, or sense that the class are starting to get tetchy and bored, it may be time for experiment. Here is a selection of activity suggestions, many of which are adaptable to any subject or age group. Some are straightforward, some are more complicated, but with such a variety of choice there can be no more excuses to over-rely on seven-year-old worksheets!

Teacher led	Student led
• Teacher talks/gives instructions • Teacher models an idea/activity • Teacher leads question/answer session • Teacher writes information on board for class to copy • Teacher writes student ideas on board • Teacher gives a demonstration	• Students give individual/group presentations to class • Students brainstorm for ideas • Students ask teacher questions (good for revision) • Students explain an idea/concept in their own words • Students do example questions on board

Reading	Writing
• Shared reading (whole class) • Individual, quiet reading • Fiction/non-fiction/newspapers/textbooks/plays/poetry/letters • Reading out their work • Reading each other's work • Reading for information • Reading for understanding • Skim reading • Reading for analysis of writing style, structure or content • Reading for enjoyment	• Descriptive writing (e.g. character profiles) • Imaginative writing (stories, plays, poetry, cartoon strips) • Factual writing (formal letters, reports, instructions, articles) • Persuasive writing (leaflets, posters, speeches, adverts) • Writing a summary • Essays • Using writing frameworks for structuring work • Handwriting tasks • Answering questions from the board/textbook

Speaking and listening	Visual
• Group discussions • Debates • Question and answer sessions • Oral presentations • Listening exercises (using tapes) • Circle time • Quizzes • Quick-fire general knowledge/ revision questions	• Interpreting images (photos, posters, paintings) for meaning • Using images as stimulus for creative work • Using images to convey ideas • (e.g. historical events, geographical location) • Watching film, television footage • Studying objects and artefacts

Practical	Experience led
• Performance of role-plays, dance, drama, physical exercises • Carrying out experiments • Designing and testing • Demonstrations (e.g. showing the class how to use a compass) • Using tools and other equipment	• Being part of an event or happening (e.g. going on trips) • Hearing a guest speaker • Re-enacting a historical period or event within the classroom (through role-play, room decoration or costume) • Using sensory stimulus (e.g. music, light, noise, taste) to inspire or reinforce ideas

New technology	Creative
• Using ICT to produce work (e.g. word-processing, graphics) • Presentations using interactive white board • ICT-based projects using computer programs (e.g. PowerPoint) • Designing a class website • Researching information on the net • Using digital film/photographs to record class activities	• Drawing exercises (from life or photographs) • Diagrams • Imaginative drawing • Drawing based on description (e.g. of a character in a book) • Craft activities (making cards, decorations, book covers, etc.) • Model making • Painting • Poster/leaflet design (for an event or concert)

Finding the solution

Something you will discover, as you progress with your teaching, is that strategies and activities do not always have the same effect on every student. What has been extremely successful with one class may not work with another. Or sometimes, what has worked with a certain group in the past may begin to lose its effectiveness over time. I once worked with a teacher who had tried every trick in the book to manage a child with ADHD – points charts, sticker charts, star charts, rewards and consequences, verbal warnings, regular praise. Each strategy worked brilliantly for a few weeks, and then the magic wore off – the old problems returned.

If you are in this situation with any of your students you have my sympathy – the absolute frustration of feeling as though you cannot get through to them. The last thing you should do, however, is give up. The best strategy for dealing with those who seem to evade strategies is to have lots of strategies, and lots of dialogue between yourself, the student, the parents and other teachers, so that you can begin to work out what truly motivates that individual. Incentives and disincentives need to have real meaning to them if they are to be effective.

Sometimes it can seem as if a student is simply not in touch with their motivations (those that 'don't care' or 'can't be bothered'). Finding out how to get through to them can be a long investigative process of trial and error, so having lots of strategies up your sleeve means you have other options when one seems to be failing. For instance, an individual reward system that has lost its charm – start by asking yourself a few questions:

- Has the strategy had enough time to make a difference?
- Has the strategy been applied fairly and consistently?
- Does the student fully understand what is expected of them?
- Is the strategy appropriate to the needs, interests and age of the student?

There are no overnight miracle cures. Behaviour improvement is a slow-burner, so it is imperative that you do not lose patience too quickly. If, however, your honest answers to the above questions are all yes, you will need to look at how you can change your approach. Perhaps the student will respond to shorter, sharper consequences? Immediate withdrawal or loss of privileges? A different tone (firmer, softer, more light-hearted)? More frequent rewards? Other incentives (getting to choose a favoured activity, time on the computer, a comment in their planner, a phone call home)? If you feel stuck for ideas talk to other staff, consider finding some training, or try some of the suggestions in this book.

23 Raising achievement

Challenging your students

As a worldly-wise teacher, you will know that your remit is not just to get your students to achieve academically – it is to *raise* their achievement. To get them to do as well as they possibly can. This is no small feat, given the hurdles faced by the average mainstream classroom, but it also has the potential to be one of the most rewarding aspects of the job. (I am convinced my physics teacher shed tears of joy when my predicted 'F' turned into an earth-staggering 'D'!)

The most important underlying facet of raising achievement is the level of challenge that you provide for your students. If you get this right you will create a learning environment that builds their confidence, keeps them interested and continuously pushes them forward. The biggest stumbling block is the fact that, despite streaming, banding and ability grouping, individual students work at individual paces and have individual needs and abilities. Inevitably, some will be ahead and others will be behind. It is not an insurmountable problem, but it may create more work for you in terms of differentiation.

Fortunately, creating a suitably challenging learning environment for your students is not just about the level of work they are given. There are other ways in which you can give them an enriching, motivating and mind-expanding experience:

- *Give them high expectations of themselves*: Tell your students, no matter what level they are at, that you have confidence in their potential. Regularly talk to them about their aims and motivations, and explain how education can help them to achieve their goals. Encourage them to understand that mistakes and struggles are not just acceptable but are actually very useful in helping us learn – they should not be deterred by challenge.

Give acknowledgement and praise for any effort and progress that is made.

- *Encourage them to think laterally*: If you can be a bit creative in the way you plan and structure your lessons you will be able to surprise and stimulate, and encourage your students to explore ideas for themselves. Try not to spoon-feed information to them – give them a few cues (such as images, objects or text) that can be used to generate discussion and interpretation. Encourage them to recognize the way in which different subjects and ideas are connected – history, geography, languages, art, religion, etc.
- *Encourage them to challenge opinions and ideas*: Whether from your mouth, a textbook, their own understanding or the widely accepted truth – remind your students that knowledge can and should be challenged. We once thought that women who enjoyed herb gardens were witches. Nowadays, herbal remedies are a widely accepted form of alternative medicine. If education is the future, surely the curriculum should be hell-bent on nurturing individuals who can think for themselves, and step outside of the religious, social and political doctrines that cause so many problems in our world?

Setting targets

In order to raise achievement you will need to make your academic expectations of your students explicit. A simple way to do this is to set them targets, giving them clear aims to work towards. Targets enable you to break learning objectives down into smaller, manageable chunks, and can be a powerful motivational force, encouraging students to be aware of the progress they are making.

Although it may not be possible to set and review specific targets for every individual student at every step of the way, there will be certain individuals who may really benefit from this kind of personalized input: those with low self-esteem or learning needs. Otherwise, targets can be general, applying to a whole class or group of students. Consider displaying targets around the room, to serve as visual reminders. They could be changed weekly, focusing on different subjects or issues: 'Our numeracy target for this week: to learn our four times table.' It may be necessary to differentiate targets within the classroom, so that they are meaningful to students with differing needs and abilities. If a target is unattainable it is more likely to discourage than motivate. Helpful targets need to be:

1. *Meaningful:* the student needs to be made aware of them, and interested in achieving them (is there a reward?).
2. *Achievable:* look at ways of breaking learning objectives into small steps that can be identified as 'milestones' of progress.
3. *Specific:* they need to clear, simple and succinct, for example: 'Use capital letters at the start of each new sentence' as opposed to 'Improve punctuation'.
4. *Measurable:* both you and the student need to be able to identify that a target has been reached, so try to include criteria for measurement (for example: 'To answer at least seven out of ten questions right in end-of-week test').
5. *Time-restricted:* if targets are not frequently reviewed or changed they lose impact. They can always be repeated if they are not achieved first time round. If a target consistently fails to be achieved, the target itself may need to be reconsidered.

Using assessment

Where your students get to will generally depend on where they have started from, but you can help to nurture this process of development by keeping a close eye on their progress. Assessment, both formal and informal, can help you to fine-tune your understanding of this journey, and find the right targets to aim for. Of course, quality assessment takes time – and time is not your friend when you work in a busy school, so make sure the effort you put in is going to be useful to you.

There are different ways of carrying out assessment (see Part One for ideas), and they serve different masters. Some forms of assessment are valuable to you, giving you insight into what your students need to know in order to progress to new levels. Some are more for the benefit of others: students, parents, government statistics and anyone who likes to see results on the table. I am not negating the importance of this – indeed, receiving good grades can be very motivating for students, and certainly a record of marks proves useful when writing reports about children whose faces you cannot quite remember. But too much time spent worrying about squeezing essays into grade brackets, at the expense of real insight into a student's progress, can be limiting.

Make marking and assessment purposeful to you, so that it can be used to inform your understanding of student progress and help you to plan for their needs. Perhaps quality is more important than quantity? Ten minutes' thoughtful analysis of a student's folder of work – identifying recurring mistakes, gaps in knowledge, misunderstanding of ideas/vocabulary, areas of uncertainty, and improvements, is worth two hours of mindless essay marking, where one piece of work becomes indistinguishable from the next and none of the useful information is retained.

Part Nine
Remaining Positive

For all the benefits that several years of experience bring – increased confidence, reduced stress, a streamlined workload – you may still find yourself waking up in the morning thinking, 'Why do I do this to myself every day?' As much as I like to extol the joys and virtues of teaching, I am utterly aware that it is just a job. While it is possible to love this job, I am sure many teachers would happily think of other things they could be doing, should they no longer have to earn money! If you sometimes feel negative about teaching, do not worry – it is quite normal. If you often feel negative about teaching, the same applies (we're not perfect). If you *always* feel negative about teaching, that is a different matter. Perhaps it is time for a career rethink?

But before you give up entirely, remind yourself that something is only as awful as your perception of it. If you are having a bad day, take a moment to ponder this idea. What is making it bad? Often the answer lies within. Perhaps you have taught one 'Spanish Armada' lesson too many? Perhaps you are feeling as though no one appreciates the effort you make? Maybe you are worrying about that enormous 'to do' list? Or blaming yourself for the student who misbehaved? This part of the book deals with the downward cycles that can dampen, and eventually destroy, your enthusiasm for the job – teaching 'ruts'. All together now: 'WE LOVE TEACHING! WE LOVE TEACHING!'

24 Teaching 'ruts'

Keeping it fresh

The downside of becoming confident and competent at what you do is that you can sometimes start to lose the 'edge' which keeps you on your toes. The tension and adrenalin that is needed to carry you through your early years in the classroom is no longer required . . . into the comfort zone. For some people comfort/easy equates with boredom. Fortunately there are plenty of things you can do to avoid a state of stagnation and renew your enthusiasm:

- *Change your schemes of work*: If your lessons seem a little lacklustre, revive the content by adjusting or rewriting your schemes of work. Of course there are limits (that damn prescriptive curriculum we all moan about), but the choice of activities and the angle you choose to approach a topic from can be refreshed. Take a few risks, try new methods and surprise yourself as well as your students.
- *Give yourself new challenges*: Do something that gives you a different perspective on school life, or takes you out of that comfort zone. Offer to direct a school play, join the orchestra or organize an outdoor pursuits week – whatever interests you. The contributions that are made to wider school life are some of the most rewarding – as well as allowing you to indulge in new or favourite pastimes.
- *Focus on a particular responsibility*: Channel your unused energies into developing an understanding of some of the many student needs that may have flashed all too quickly past your eyes as a busy new teacher. Some of these needs are very interesting: gifted and talented, autism, ADD/ADHD or dyslexia, for example. Deepening your understanding, through observation

and analysis, training or research, will not only stimulate interest but will improve your classroom relationships.

- *Teach a different year group*: If you are bogged down by GCSE
  coursework, or frustrated with year 8 apathy, a few hours a
  week with some meek year 7 'babies' may appease you. Or if
  you are a Key Stage 1 teacher who is sick of the tantrums, try
  some suave and sophisticated year 6s for size! A change is as
  good as a rest they say. If you think a change of year group
  may be the challenge you are looking for, discuss the possi-
  bility with your head of department.
- *Try a different subject*: In most schools the timetable offers some
  flexibility to those who pursue it. If you have experience, or
  even just an interest in a particular subject, you may be able
  to take it on as a subsidiary. I once knew a religious studies
  teacher who set up a thriving media studies department, complete with film equipment and editing suite.

Feeling valued

For many people a major motivational factor in the work place is the
acknowledgement and appreciation of their efforts. Unfortunately,
being told what a wonderful, important job you are doing is an all
too rare occurrence in the teaching profession. Sometimes you will
only discover how grateful everyone is when your time is up. Your
leaving presentation: '. . . and who could forget her unwavering
efforts in the school vegetable patch'; or the obligatory box of chocs
and squeaky voice: 'My mum says I've got to say "thankyou" for
being my teacher in Class 5.'

A continuous stream of ungrateful students, inconsiderate staff
members, impatient parents and media blasts may gradually drain
your egalitarian commitment to the teaching profession. Relish the
precious moments when you do feel valued, and if encouragement
and recognition is not your manager's management style, politely
ask them – praise and gratitude is not just about ego boosting, it is
inspirational and reassuring. If management want the best from
their staff, they need to make them feel as though they are capable
of giving 'the best'.

Do you value yourself? Teachers spend so much time focusing
on the achievement and progress that they are enabling others to

make: helping students to read and write, getting them through exams, encouraging them to discover life. This can be a powerful source of personal satisfaction – the knowledge that you have guided, shaped and formed the minds of a group of young people can be very rewarding. If those young people experience success the rewards can be particularly great. However, not all students go in the direction we want them to, and for some teachers the struggles outweigh the progress. In these circumstances you can at least look to your own strengths as a source of pride and comfort: your determination, your resilience, your commitment.

One of the curious wonders of teaching is that, despite playing a pivotal role in the lives of your students, you may never know what impact you have on them. Maybe your name and face is popping up in the thoughts of bankers, artists, scientists, and sports-people everywhere – but will that legacy ever be known to you? Sure enough, one day you will be quietly waiting for the number 20, working a tricky crossword clue in your mind while keeping one eye on your shopping, when you are blind-sided by a brash and overfamiliar voice, 'All right Miss, remember me?' You turn to see a plump, shaggy-haired girl, early 20s, casually herding three gap-toothed boys. Remember her? How could you forget? The arguments. The lies. The attitude. (And as you stand there open-mouthed, trying to look pleasantly surprised, her youngest catches your attention: from behind a perfectly poised index finger is that very same knowing grin.)

Challenging negativity

Unfortunately, the teaching profession is frequently dogged by negativity. Concerns over how we protect, discipline, support and even feed our young people, combined with the very public scrutiny of school standards, create enormous pressures for staff. If the general consensus is that schools are battling, while teachers are overburdened and underappreciated (despite what the adverts tell us), is it any wonder that we have difficulties regarding teacher recruitment and retention?

For the critics, teachers are an easy scapegoat for society and all its ills. When children misbehave or fail to pass exams the finger points straight to schools and those who work in them. Of course, schools have a responsibility to address these issues, but they are only part of the equation: they rely on funding, support, resources, training, and investment from both the government and the communities they provide for – and I have yet to meet a teacher who believes that all of these things are adequately in place.

For some teachers the reality of working in education is far more palpable than its stigma, but for many it really is tough. This does not, however, need to be a knell of doom. Education's problems may not go away easily or quietly, but they will definitely not go away if we give up on them. I have always been impressed by the amount of effort and commitment made by the staff I have worked with. Teachers may have a reputation for constant whingeing, but in my experience, they are pragmatists – there is no time to stand about and complain!

So how do you see past the obstacles, view your daily toil positively and achieve job satisfaction? Start by ignoring the staffroom dinosaurs, the bitter has-beens who cling to their antique canes while griping about declining standards – they are not the future of education. Remind yourself that the responsibility does not rest entirely on your shoulders. Yes, you have a duty to manage the behaviour and development of your students, but you cannot make their choices for them.

Avoiding 'burn out'

In such a demanding job it is easy to tire yourself – the feeling of being worn down, or 'burnt out', is an all too common teacher complaint. Although many would suggest that your first year is likely to be the most tiring, be aware that it is a job which grows with you. After five years you may find yourself with more responsibility, more stress and less time than ever. If you wish for longevity in the teaching profession it is important that you learn to respect your physical and emotional needs and take steps to avoid pushing yourself too hard too much of the time. There are a few things you can do to protect yourself from exhaustion:

- *Pace yourself.* Take a few minutes to reflect on your yearly timetable. When are your busiest times (reports due, coursework in, etc.) and your quietest ones (students on study

leave/work experience)? Knowing what to expect will help
you to prepare mentally for the busy times, and will allow you
to do some early groundwork before it gets too hectic (for
example, organizing your marking and assessment, in preparation for report writing).

- *Take your breaks*: Lunch and break times can easily be swallowed
  up by a large workload – duties, paperwork, extra-curricular
  activities or detentions. But if anything in a teacher's day
  should be sacred it is the opportunity to escape from the sight
  (if not the sound) of the students for a short while, and relax
  with a hot drink/chat/practical joke/magazine/snack. Treat
  your breaks as a priority – your stamina, and your feet, will
  thank you for it.
- *Learn to say 'no'*: Do not be surprised if other staff members
  constantly seek your help, assistance or contributions. Can
  you direct the school musical this year? Can you use your
  artistic flair on these displays? Can you show these students
  how to build their own calculator? Of course it is flattering to
  know that your skills are so valued, but be careful: if you show
  willing, at first, people will be grateful; then, they will take
  advantage. Only agree to do the things that a) your really want
  to, and b) you can truly manage: 'I would love to help out,
  but unfortunately I just don't have the time at the moment.'
- *Know your limits*: Be aware of your physical and emotional
  states of health. If either of them seem a bit rocky, make some
  temporary cutbacks and allow yourself to recover. Deliver
  some 'easy' lessons (videos, student presentations, a 'test'),
  leave school as early as possible each day, skip homework for
  a week (reducing your marking), and use any time gained to
  pamper yourself.

Part Ten

Career Progression

Once you have tamed the beast of classroom teaching you may feel ready to take on more responsibility or broaden your experience in a particular area. A career in education provides a structured passport to promotion, although the frequency of opportunities can be somewhat limited. If the teaching population in your school is stable you may have to wait some time before the right opportunity comes up or, alternatively, look elsewhere. If, on the other hand, your school has a high turnover of staff, promotion opportunities will probably be thrust upon you as soon as you are able to speak and write at the same time!

Whether you have your sights set on a headship, or would prefer to stay closer to the classroom, there are a number of ways in which you can increase your status, salary and job satisfaction. The job will grow with you. This part of the book looks at the possibilities, pros and cons of developing your school career, and also reflects on the wider choices that are available to you: your prospects beyond the school gates.

25 Exploring your options

Specializing

With a variety of options available to you it can be difficult to know which way to turn or what pathway to take. But after a few years in the classroom you should have a fairly reasonable insight into what aspects of the job you enjoy, or have an interest in: pastoral care, special needs or curriculum matters, for example. Here is a table of possible opportunities or specialisms within both schools and education at large. (The opportunities available to you may vary according to your school or authority, and job titles may also differ. The '*' denotes jobs that are potentially non-school based.)

Pastoral	Curriculum
• Class tutor • School counsellor • Educational welfare officer* • Home–school liaison support* • Child protection officer* • Head of careers/work experience • Deputy head of year • Head of year • Head of pastoral care	• Deputy head of department • Head of department • Key Stage coordinator • Head of faculty • Curriculum adviser* • Key Stage adviser*

Senior teachers/Leadership	Special needs
• Deputy headteacher • Headteacher • School governor • Senior teacher with special responsibility (e.g. timetable,	• EAL support teacher • Gifted and talented coordinator • Teacher of SEN (mainstream, special schools or units) • Teacher of learning support

Senior teachers/Leadership	Special needs
attendance, examinations, school events, health and safety, finance)	• Head of learning support • Assistant SENCO • SENCO • Special needs officer★ • Educational psychologist★

Behaviour	Classroom
• Behaviour support teacher • Deputy head of behaviour support • Head of behaviour support • Advisory teacher★ • Teacher in a PRU (Pupil Referral Unit) • Head of PRU	• Advanced skills teacher • Threshold payment • Subject mentor • Float teacher • Supply teacher

Training	Strategic planning/other
• Subject mentor (for trainee teachers/NQTs) • INSET provider★ • Lecturing★ • Teacher training★ • Teacher assessment★	• Local authority administration★ • DfES★ • Minister for education★ • Secretary of state for education★ • Ofsted inspector★ • Education consultancy★ • Research★ • Educational writer★

Increasing your responsibility

Schools are generally keen to find ways of giving young teachers more money (thus increasing the chances of retaining them), and will come up with all sorts of inventive ways to bolster your salary with further responsibility points. This can be very helpful – a few more pay increments are always welcome (if not *needed*). Occasionally management may try to hound you into taking on a role you simply do not want. Resistance can be difficult: if you say no now, what will happen when something comes along that you actually do want? But if they want you more than you want their job, at least you have the bargaining power. Be firm and explicit about your expectations (money matters, proper support, adequate training) – and if they say 'temporary' make sure they *mean* temporary.

If you feel you are ready to explore new challenges, begin by asking yourself these questions:

- *What are your areas of interest?* Do you like interacting and building relationships with your students? Do you enjoy organizing and working within your staff team? Are you dedicated to your subject? Whatever your interests are, your chances of future job satisfaction increase if they form the basis of your career development. There is little point in becoming a head of year if you actively hate chasing up students and dealing with their problems.
- *What are your long-term goals?* For some, it is easy to picture where they would like to be at the height of their career. For others, the future is a mystery. If you do have particular goals the choices you make along the way will help (or hinder) your chances. Talk to the people who have got to where you want to be, and find out what sort of experience will help you.
- *What are your short-term goals?* Ambitions are more easily achieved if the efforts to get there are broken down into smaller steps. So you are a Reception teacher wanting to run your own nursery – what skills and experience will you need to accrue in order to be successful? The next logical step might be running a parents' club (experience of dealing with significant others), a curriculum responsibility (the chance to handle a budget), or a training responsibility (managing people).
- *What level of responsibility do you want your next step to give you?* Short-term goals also need to reflect your current needs. If you are enjoying the classroom, do you really want to be taken away from it for a substantial amount of the week? If you still feel uncertain about your strengths, are you ready for additional pressures? Or are you itching to get out of the classroom and into a new role?
- *What opportunities are currently available?* Listen out for any internal opportunities that come up but, if you are desperate for a quick promotion, accept that you may have to look elsewhere. And remember, it never hurts to ask. If you see an opportunity, or discover a way in which you can make yourself useful, invent a role for yourself and see what they say!

Staying where you are

If you are happy in the classroom and displeased by the thought of having additional responsibilities, you may not be inclined to pursue promotion – but the desire to remain a classroom teacher does not mean a career stops progressing. Each year you will move up the pay scale, enrich your experience and further your understanding. You will encounter new students, new ideas, new issues and new solutions to old problems.

If you get to the point where you would like more challenge (and more money), while remaining in the classroom, you may be eligible to become an advanced skills teacher. This title will acknowledge your talents within the classroom, and place you on a higher pay scale. Advanced skills teachers may have expertise within a particular subject or area, and will be required to spread their wisdom around the school. Another option is applying for the threshold entitlement.

In some schools there can be quite a lot of pressure on staff to apply for promotion or take on further responsibility. If you demonstrate capability the chances are you will be earmarked for something or other. Great if this is what you want, but unwelcome pressure if it is not. So if you want them to leave you alone, pretend to be really bad at your job – but not so bad that you get fired!

Dealing with a new role

A further set of responsibilities will inevitably have an effect on your experience of school life. Maybe your timetable will be altered, or your contact with staff and students reduced. Your administrative duties may increase, and perhaps you will need to attend more meetings. Your expectations of yourself will change, but so too will the expectations of those around you: your managers and your 'underlings'. Consider how it might feel to have senior staff make demands on you as an equal, and trust you to fulfil important obligations with little or no holding of your hand. How would you cope with other colleagues frequently coming to you for assistance and instruction: can you deal with this student/can you call that one's parents? With promotion, particularly towards management, you may find yourself becoming increasingly answerable and accountable.

Hopefully, your new role will be well supported, with experienced staff nurturing your confidence and providing 'Obi-wan'-style mentoring – but ultimately it is down to you to raise your game and embrace the challenges. Are you ready for them? One of the most important aspects of managerial responsibility is dealing with staff (as well as students), which can be difficult and highly stressful. You may have to change the way you relate to other teachers. What if some of your 'friends' are not doing their job properly? Can you balance social camaraderie with your managerial persona? Can you deal with resentment – backstabbing from other staff who may have wanted your promotion for themselves?

As a manager, you will also have to review the way you relate to your students. You may find yourself spending more time dealing with problems, and less time working with the charming and motivated. You will also have to be more conscious of the way you project yourself. A head of year, for example, will need to have an authoritative identity – someone who can handle student misbehaviour and inspire respect. This persona will need to be maintained all around school.

26 Change

Starting a new school

Your school is bound to contain at least one teacher who has been there since the 1970s, but others will come and go. If you, yourself, are feeling a little jaded, or in need of refreshment, perhaps it is time for a change? A new challenge or environment can inspire an entirely different attitude to work, so start flicking through the sometimes mammoth jobs section of the *TES* and see what is on offer.

Job searches fall into three categories: the 'I'll take anything, just get me out of here!' ones, the 'I know exactly what I want' ones, and the speculative/aspirational ones (happy where you are, but if the right opportunity were to come along . . .). There are many different reasons why you may require or benefit from change: more money, better prospects, promotion, a new location, convenient travel, a different 'type' of school, new students, new colleagues . . .

Whatever your reasons for moving on, it is important to remember that different schools will have different atmospheres, and different ways of doing things. You may have to accept and get used to unfamiliar systems – there is nothing more irritating than the new teacher who constantly comments on how much better their old school did things (if it was so great, why did they leave?). If you have moved to another area you may also have to adjust to different accents or attitudes. But, ultimately, a change of school can inject your career with enthusiasm, and will give you the chance to encounter new things and broaden your experience. For hints and ideas on job applications and interview preparation see Part Three: Coping with Your First Job.

Taking a career break

Perhaps the change you are looking for is more dramatic than simply taking a job in another school. There are (hopefully) many more facets to your life beyond work, but some of these may not sit comfortable alongside the daily toil. Starting a family, foreign travel, fulfilling a creative ambition, further study, or perhaps teaching abroad – important life goals that require dedicated time. Although the school holidays provide a certain amount of freedom, individual plans may extend further. If your life's ambition is to backpack around the world, squashing five continents into five weeks is unlikely to satisfy that desire.

Giving up the classroom for a temporary change of scenery can also have a positive effect on your approach to work, renewing your interest and allowing you to get some perspective on your circumstances. As someone who has taken time out of teaching (first to do the aforementioned backpack and world effort and, years later, to write this masterpiece!), I am a hearty advocate of career breaks. As a result, life has felt fuller; and this, in turn, has enabled me to enjoy and value the classroom in a different way. I no longer feel interminably bound to it or defined by it, and because of this I am able to appreciate it for what it is.

If you *are* considering a career break there are a few things you will need to take into consideration. Although it is increasingly acceptable these days (some schools will even hold a job open for you, or make promises for your return), decisions should not be made in haste. How will leaving your current job affect your long-term career prospects? Will it be easy for you to return to the same/another desirable job? What are the financial implications going to be? And, of course, you may need to consider how a break will affect your personal attitude to work. If your decision to leave is in any way motivated by unhappiness with your job, how easy will it be to return? Time away from the classroom will mean losing touch with your practice, so getting back into the saddle could prove stressful.

Giving yourself flexibility

The other option available to those seeking improved work–life balance is taking a part-time position or job share (although opportunities are fairly rare). Although part-time work means part-time money, it does allow you to liberate several days of the week while maintaining all the benefits of a permanent position: regular income, regular routines, regular students and regular colleague camaraderie. You can still 'belong' to the school, but with a part-time commitment.

Alternatively, you may choose to pursue supply work: day to day, short or long term. There are plenty of agencies eager to get you on their books, and take on the responsibility of finding you work (as well as a cut of the money for themselves). Although potentially a great way of earning money from your craft while giving you flexibility, take heed: casual supply seems to be on the decline. If you do not wish to make a long-term commitment to a school (for example maternity cover), you may struggle if you have to rely on it financially. The idea that you can 'choose your hours' is a bit of myth – more likely is it that you will take what you can get.

The other significant downside to supply work is the inevitable lack of consistency that you will experience. If you are lucky enough to get regular work in the same establishment(s) this becomes less of a problem. If not, then you will have to be prepared for some tough situations. Chasing people up, finding resources and suitable lessons plans, following procedures, and having an impact on student behaviour – these things can be difficult to achieve if you do not know the class, the class teacher or the school. It is no wonder that students are famous for playing up in the presence of supply teachers – effective behaviour management is dependent upon *relationships*, and these require time to develop. You need to get to know them, and they need to get to know you.

Do not be surprised if much of the work you are offered is in schools that are having difficulties, particularly regarding student discipline. Unfortunately, the kind of environments that would really benefit from strong, consistent teacher presence often have problems (unsurprisingly) with staff retention: cue the revolving door for supply teachers. And so the students that are most in need of firm support and structure have no consistent provision for weeks, months or, sometimes, terms – the problems are compounded.

There is no denying that supply work can be difficult, but maybe that matters less when you know you can easily and quietly walk away from it. The flipside of the supply coin: no hefty responsibilities, no monster workloads, and if you find yourself at the mercy of a terrible place, you need never return.

Transferring your skills

For some, the only way to cope with a career in teaching is to leave. Avoid making judgements within your first few years – it *does* get easier. But if, after all the struggles and strains, you have decided that life in the classroom is really not for you, walking out of the school gates for the final time should bring immediate relief. Admitting defeat – perhaps you are choosing to leave because you cannot cope with the pressure, or have been worn down by difficult behaviour – can leave you feeling demoralized and unsure of yourself. You trained hard for the qualification. You ploughed effort and energy into the job, yet all it has given you is a headache and a sore throat. Maybe you are leaving because you have simply realized your interests lie elsewhere. Whether the factors behind your decision are pushing or pulling you, trust your instincts and focus on the new opportunities that lie head of you. And try not to regret your experience of the classroom – if nothing else, you will have learned from it.

Teaching, although a unique talent in itself, is really a combination of different skills. Many of these will be transferable and, indeed, desirable in other career pathways. Whether you have managed two, five or ten years in the classroom, reflect on what you have gained:

- flexibility
- organizational skills
- ability to think on your feet
- communication skills
- presentation skills
- confidence in front of large groups
- problem solving
- multi-tasking
- time management
- teamwork
- remaining calm in the face of challenge
- coping with pressure

- creativity
- motivating others
- managing people
- project planning
- financial management.

Conclusion

So here ends my teaching odyssey – no crackpot theories, no wacky diagrams, just good old common sense, practical advice and a little bit of empathy. Five years in teaching, and you don't look a day older! Hopefully this guide has served you well, and raised a smile or two. I also hope it has felt like a trustworthy companion, an honest account of what life is like in the world of teaching. We are constantly surrounded by myths, misrepresentations and lies about what our profession is and is not. The media, the government, the parents, the students – all want to have their say over the way we do things. But ultimately we are the ones in the front line. We know it's not easy, we know it's not perfect, but it is ours. We can, and should, make the most of it. Good luck, and here's to the next five years!

Index